Philip

Piranha

T0248968

Bloomsbury Methuen Drama
An imprint of Bloomsbury Publishing Plc

B L O O M S B U R Y
LONDON · NEW DELHI · NEW YORK · SYDNEY

Bloomsbury Methuen Drama

An imprint of Bloomsbury Publishing Plc

Imprint previously known as Methuen Drama

50 Bedford Square	1385 Broadway
London	New York
WC1B 3DP	NY 10018
UK	USA

www.bloomsbury.com

BLOOMSBURY, METHUEN DRAMA **and the Diana logo
are trademarks of Bloomsbury Publishing Plc**

First published 2008
This edition published in 2015

© Philip Ridley, 2008, 2015

British Library Cataloguing-in-Publication Data
A catalogue record for this book is available from the British Library

ISBN: PB: 978-1-4742-3884-7
ePDF: 978-1-4742-3886-1
ePub: 978-1-4742-3885-4

Library of Congress Cataloging-in-Publication Data
A catalog record for this book is available from the Library of Congress

Series: Modern Plays

Typeset by Country Setting, Kingsdown, Kent CT14 8ES

OLD RED LION THEATRE

EXCEPTIONAL THEATRE IN
THE HEART OF ISLINGTON

D.E.M. Productions presents

PIRANHA HEIGHTS

by Philip Ridley

11 November–6 December 2014

Box Office: 0844 412 4307

Old Red Lion Theatre
418 St John Street
London EC1V 4NJ

http://www.oldredliontheatre.co.uk/

Cast

(in order of appearance)

Alan	**Alex Lowe**
Terry	**Phil Cheadle**
Lilly	**Rebecca Boey**
Medic	**Ryan Gerald**
Garth	**Jassa Ahluwalia**

Crew

Max Barton	Director
Cécile Trémolières	Designer
Paul McLeish	Lighting Designer
Rhys Lewis	Sound Designer/Composer
Ramin Sabi	Producer
Oliver King	Co-Producer
Leyla McLennan	Co-Producer
Harriet May	Production and Stage Manager
Esmé Hicks	Assistant Director
Sheridan Humphreys	PR
Tom Powell	Marketing Manager
Rachel Carter	Production Assistant
Georgia Clemson	Production Assistant

Cast

Alex Lowe | Alan

Alex's television work includes the upcoming BBC/HBO adaptation of J. K. Rowling's *The Casual Vacancy*, *The Thick of It*, *Pompidou*, *Toast Napoleon*, *Still Open All Hours*, and *Judge John Deed* (BBC), *Peep Show*, *Orphans*, *Phoenix Nights* and *Spaced* (Channel 4), *Secret Diary of a Call Girl* and *Midsomer Murders* (ITV). His film work includes the upcoming Sasha Baron Cohen project *Grimsby/The Curse of Hendon*; previously: *My Week with Marilyn*, (Weinstein), *Peter's Friends* and *Much Ado About Nothing*, both directed by Kenneth Branagh. Recent theatre work includes *Fatal Attraction* directed by Trevor Nunn at Theatre Royal Haymarket, *The Changeling* (Young Vic), *The Girlfriend Experience* (Royal Court), *Dennis the Menace* (South Bank Centre) and *Charley's Aunt* (Worcester Swan Theatre).

Jassa Ahluwalia | Garth

Jassa's breakthrough role was as Rocky on BBC3's *Some Girls* (Hat Trick Productions). Other television includes *Ripper Street* (BBC1), *The Whale* (BBC Worldwide), and *The Bible* (Lightworkers Media). Film includes leading roles in *Generation Z* (Matador Pictures), to be released next year, *DragonHeart: The Sorcerer's Curse* (Universal), *Resistance* (Big Rich Films), *Assessment* (UK Film Council), *My Angel* (CKM Entertainment), and *Journey to the Moon* (Dream On Films). Stage work includes the leads in *Peter Pan* (Camberley Theatre), *Treasure Island* (Derek Grant Organisation) and *Aladdin* (Blue Genie Entertainment). Producing work includes the short film *Modern Man*, an official selection at the San Diego Film Festival 2014, winner of Best Film at Kinofilm Manchester (12th International Short Film Festival) and winner of Best Comedy Short at the Isle of Man Film Festival 2014.

Phil Cheadle | Terry

Phil trained at RADA. His theatre includes: *Variation on a Theme, Events While Guarding the Bofors Gun* (Finborough Theatre); *Mrs. Affleck* (National Theatre); *Henry IV Part I, Henry IV Part II, Bedlam* (Shakespeare's Globe Theatre); *The Changeling* (Cheek by Jowl); *Dear Uncle, Neighbourhood Watch* (Stephen Joseph Theatre/59E59 Street Theatre, NY); *Blue Remembered Hills* (Northern Stage); *Strawberry Fields* by Alecky Blythe (Pentabus); *All My Sons* (Leicester Curve); *Far from the Madding Crowd* (ETT); *Macbeth* (West Yorkshire Playhouse); *Knives in Hens, Tartuffe* (Arcola); *If I Were You* (Manchester Library Theatre); *The Tempest, St Joan* (AandBC Productions, US tour); *As You Like It* (Northcott). Television: *Crimson Fields, New Worlds, Silent Witness, Inspector Lynley, Inside the Titanic, Coronation Street, Hollyoaks.* Film: *John Carter, Comes a Bright Day, To the Sea.*

Rebecca Boey | Lilly

Rebecca Boey trained at East 15 and is a graduate of the Royal Court Young Writers' Programme. Theatre credits include *Crystal Springs* (Park Theatre), *From Russia for Love* (Theatre Delicatessen), *Island* (National Theatre), *Skin* (Arcola), *Sihanoukville* (Finborough Theatre), *Ken Campbell's School of Night* (Latitude), and *The One Hour Plays* (Underbelly, Canal Café, London Zoo and Latitude.) Film credits include the feature film *Schadenfreude* (Mutant Robot Productions), currently in production, and short films *Aristocracy* (Transcend Pictures,) *Life Ever After* (Jackdaw Studios) and *Full* (B3 Media for BBC Writersroom).

Ryan Gerald | Medic

Ryan attended Guildford School of Acting and undertook the three-year BA acting course, graduating in 2012. Shortly after graduating, Ryan toured the UK with the play *Blue/Orange*. Film credits include Jay in the short film *Streets in the Sky* (BFI/Film London) and Chris Boas in *Jus Soli* (SomebodyNobody Productions). Theatre credits include Ninja in *Tower Block* (Ministry of Stories), *Soldier* in Owen Wingrave (Aldeburgh Music and Edinburgh Festival).

Philip Ridley | Writer

Philip was born in the East End of London where he still lives and works. He studied painting at St Martin's School of Art and his work has been exhibited widely throughout Europe and Japan. As well as three books for adults – and the highly acclaimed screenplay for the *The Krays* feature film (winner of the *Evening Standard* Best Film of the Year Award) – he has written ten adult stage plays: the seminal *The Pitchfork Disney (*soon to be published as a Modern Classic by Methuen), the multi-award-winning *The Fastest Clock in the Universe, Ghost from a Perfect Place, Vincent River, Mercury Fur, Leaves of Glass, Piranha Heights, Tender Napalm* (nominated for the London Fringe Best Play Award), *Shivered* (nominated Off-West End Best New Play Award) and *Dark Vanilla Jungle* (winner of an Edinburgh Festival Fringe First Award), plus several plays for young people: *Karamazoo, Fairytaleheart, Moonfleec*e (named as one of the 50 Best Works About Cultural Diversity by the National Centre for Children's Books), *Sparkleshark* and *Brokenville* (collectively known as *The Storyteller Sequence*), and a play for the whole family, *Feathers in the Snow* (shortlisted for the Brian Way Best Play Award). He has also written books for children, including *Scribbleboy* (shortlisted for the Carnegie Medal), *Kasper in the Glitter* (nominated for the Whitbread Prize), *Mighty Fizz Chilla* (shortlisted for the Blue Peter Book of the Year Award), *ZinderZunder, Vinegar Street, Zip's Apollo* and the bestseller *Krindlekrax* (winner of both the Smarties Prize and WH Smith's Mind-Boggling Books Award), the stage play of which – adapted by Philip himself – was premiered at the Birmingham Rep Theatre in 2002. He has also directed three feature films from his own screenplays: *The Reflecting Skin* (winner of eleven international awards (including the prestigious George Sadoul Prize), *The Passion of Darkly Noon* (winner of the Best Director Prize at the Porto Film Festival) and *Heartless* (winner of the Silver Meliers Award for Best Fantasy Film). For the latter two films, Philip co-wrote a number of original songs, one of which, 'Who Will Love Me Now?' (performed by P. J. Harvey) was voted BBC Radio 1's Top Film Song of 1998 and has since been covered by the techno-house band Sunscreem (as 'Please Save Me'), becoming both a club and viral hit. In 2010 Philip, along with song-writing collaborator Nick Bicât, formed the music group Dreamskin Cradle and their first album, *Songs from Grimm*, is available on iTunes, Amazon and all major download sites. Philip is also a performance artist in his own right, and his highly charged readings of his ongoing poetry sequence *Lovesongs for Extinct Creatures* (first embarked on when he was a student) have proved increasingly popular in recent years. In 2012 *What's On Stage* named him a Jubilee Playwright (one of the most influential British writers to have emerged in the past six decades). Philip has won both the *Evening Standard*'s Most Promising Newcomer to British Film and Most Promising Playwright Awards – the only person ever to receive both prizes.

Crew

Max Barton | Director

Max is currently Associate Director at Jermyn Street Theatre and Artistic Director of The Well. He recently co-directed a season of five world premieres with Steven Berkoff at Jermyn Street entitled *Religion and Anarchy*. At the same theatre he also directed *Spoonface Steinberg* in association with Citizens Theatre, Glasgow. Max directed the first-ever promenade production of *Hamlet* at Kronborg Castle, Elsinore. Other credits include *A Midsummer Night's Dream* (European tour); *The Curse of Macbeth* (The Playhouse at the Fringe); *Metamorphosis* (C(too), Edinburgh); *Red and White* (Drama Centre); *The Shape of Things* (Corpus Playroom); *Noises Off*, *No Magic* and *Bedroom Farce* (ADC Theatre, Cambridge); *Pool (no water)* (Homerton Studio); Max trained on the directing Masters at Birkbeck, during which time he was resident assistant to Dominic Hill at the Citizens Theatre, Glasgow. He assisted Trevor Nunn on Alan Ayckbourn's *A Chorus of Disapproval* at the Harold Pinter Theatre and was Associate Director on *Fatal Attraction* at Theatre Royal Haymarket.

Cécile Trémolières | Designer

Cécile graduated from Wimbledon College of Arts in 2013. Since then, she has been one of the 12 finalists of the Linbury Prize for Stage Design, and has been awarded the Royal Opera House bursary as well as the Ideastap design graduate award 2014. Cécile has worked on diverse types of performance: opera – *La Traviata* (Haslemere Hall, 2014) and *Micromégas* (Riverside Studios, 2013); dance – *Impermanence Dance Theatre* (2014), *Room(s)* (Scottish Dance Theatre, 2013); promenade – *This is not a Slog* (Oval House, 2014), *Dream Neasden* in collaboration with the Tricycle (2014) and *Miscellany*, Rich Mix (2014); touring structures for festival – *A is for Apple* (2014), *Impermanent Theatre* (2014); and theatre – Complicité Young Company (Hackney Downs Studio, 2015), *Europe as a Theme Park* (The Yard, 2015), *Ajax* (2015) and *The Tower* (Sherman Cymru, 2015).

Paul McLeish | Lighting Designer

Paul's credits for lighting include: at the National Theatre, *Strider: The Story of a Horse*, directed by Michael Bogdanov; *The Putney Debates*, with Brian Cox; *Vamp till Ready*, directed by Sebastian Graham-Jones; *Robert Lowell, American Poet*, with Harold Pinter; *The Trackers of Oxyrhynchus*, directed and written by Tony Harrison; *Comedy Tonight: A Tribute to Roy Kinnear* (cast included Helena Bonham-Carter, Frances de la Tour, Judi Dench, Sheila Hancock and Alan Howard), directed by Frank Hauser and Trevor Nunn; *The Pied Piper*, devised and directed by Alan Cohen; *Mother Courage*, director Anthony Clark. For the Ludlow Festival: *Macbeth*, with Haydn Gwynne; *As You Like It*, with John Gordon Sinclair; and *Othello*, with Greg Hicks. Other lighting work includes: *Crimes of the Heart* at the Man in the Moon Theatre in Chelsea; *Macbeth* and *Julius Caesar* for the Anglian Open Air Shakespeare Company in several venues around the United States, India and China; *Lettice and Lovage*, with Rosemary Leach, directed by Alan Cohen; *The Merchant of Venice* for the English Shakespeare Company with Tony Haygarth; *Beatrice and Benedict* at the Royal Festival Hall with the Academy of St Martin in the Fields conducted by Sir Neville Marriner. Paul has also worked in the Cameri Theatre, Tel Aviv; the Globe Theatre in Tokyo; Epidaurus and Delphi in Greece; and the Moscow Art Theatre. Also relighting in Paris, Madrid, Milan, Vienna, Helsinki, Cologne and many of Britain's major cities. Recent design work includes Steven Berkoff's *Religion and Anarchy* (Jermyn St Theatre) and the upcoming *Oklahoma!* (St James Theatre). Paul is now the resident technician at Westminster School and also occasionally teaches lighting at Rose Bruford school and for Royal Opera House education.

Rhys Lewis | Sound Designer/Composer

Rhys is a graduate of the London Centre of Contemporary Music, where he studied a degree in songwriting and composition. Rhys works as a freelance composer for theatre, film and TV. He also writes and performs for his own project, Rhys Lewis & The Relics. Recent theatre credits include *Eye of a Needle* (Southwark Playhouse), *Long Story Short* (Charing Cross Theatre), *A Dashing Fellow* (New Diorama), *1002 Nights* (NYT, Saudi Arabia).

Ramin Sabi | Producer

Ramin set up Deus Ex Machina Productions in London in 2014 with Tony Kushner's *A Bright Room Called Day* (Southwark Playhouse) and *Lysistrata* (Edinburgh Fringe). Previous producing work includes *Dangerous Liaisons* and *The Producers* (Oxford Playhouse); *The Oresteia, Children of Oedipus, Cabaret* and *A Theory of Justice: the Musical!* (Keble O'Reilly Theatre); *Cat on a Hot Tin Roof* (Simpkins Lee Theatre); *Bug* and *Fear* (Burton Taylor Studio); a new version of Sarah Kane's *4.48 Psychosis* and the transfer of *A Theory of Justice: the Musical!* (Edinburgh Fringe Festival), which he co-wrote and was nominated for the WhatsOnStage Best New Musical award. Upcoming projects include *Stinkfoot* (The Yard), *Donkey Heart* (Trafalgar Studios) and *How I Learned to Drive* (Southwark Playhouse). Ramin has a degree in Philosophy, Politics and Economics from Oxford.

Oliver King | Co-Producer

Oliver is a graduate of Drama Centre London, and works as a producer and actor. Producing credits include *Three Sisters, Uncle Vanya* (Wyndham's), *A Dashing Fellow* (New Diorama), *A Warsaw Melody* (Arcola), *Sunstroke* (Platform Theatre), *Mary Postgate, Hansel and Gretel* (Edinburgh Festival), *A Company of Wayward Saints, A Picture of Dorian Gray* and *Another Country* (Assembly Rooms, Durham). Associate credits include *Oedipus Tyrannus* (Harare International Festival of the Arts, Zimbabwe). He is the director of Belka Productions: www.belkaproductions.co.uk.

Leyla McLennan | Co-Producer

Leyla is currently enrolled on the Creative Producing for Theatre and Live Performance MA at Birkbeck, College of London. She graduated with a BA in Law from Cambridge University in 2014. She is associate producer of Dippermouth. Producing credits include *The Duchess of Malfi* and *The Bloody Chamber* (ADC Theatre); *The King and Queen of the Universe* (Edinburgh Fringe Festival/C Aquila); *Blue/Orange* (Corpus Playroom).

Harriet May | Production and Stage Manager

Harriet graduated from the University of Birmingham in 2013, studying Drama and Theatre Arts. Theatre work includes *God's Own Country* (Edinburgh Fringe Festival); *Fatal Attraction* (Theatre Royal Haymarket); *The Secret Garden* (Edinburgh Fringe Festival); *The Two Gentlemen of Verona* and *The Two Noble Kinsmen* (Brockley Jack Theatre); *Stop the Clocks* (Tin Box Theatre UK tour); *The Stories That Shakespeare Knew* (Midlands Art Centre/ RSC Stratford-upon-Avon); *The Last Day of Judas Iscariot* (Minerva Works).

Esmé Hicks | Assistant Director

Esmé Hicks graduated in 2013 with a BA in English from Oxford University. Theatre work includes *Potsdam Quartet* (Jermyn Street Theatre), *The Matryoska Project* (Barons Court Theatre), *4.48 Psychosis* (Edinburgh Fringe Festival), *John Rawls' A Theory of Justice: the Musical!* (Edinburgh Fringe Festival), *On Approval* (Jermyn Street Theatre), *The Sunset Limited* (Michael Pilch Studio).

Sheridan Humphreys | PR

Sheridan Humphreys has worked with leading performing arts companies including Candoco Dance Company, Improbable, Mat Fraser, Theatre 503, The HandleBards and KPS Productions. She has worked with venues across the UK from major producing theatres (including Royal Court, Lyric Hammersmith, Hampstead, Birmingham Rep, Northern Stage, Hackney Empire, Citizens Glasgow) to smaller Fringe theatres and receiving houses (including Soho Theatre, Arcola Theatre, Southwark Playhouse, Oval House Theatre, Rosemary Branch), East London Dance and rural arts centres and village halls. From 2005 to 2009 she represented over 40 shows from independent producers at the Edinburgh Festival Fringe and from 2002 to 2004 and 2011 to 2014 was head of Press and Marketing at C venues at Edinburgh Festival Fringe. From 2003 to 2008 she was a Dance and Film Critic for *Kultureflash* and is also an occasional contributor to *The Stage*.

Tom Powell | Marketing Manager

Tom Powell is an award-winning writer and producer. As an undergraduate, he won the OTR National Radio Drama Award for *Old Edward*, and the Cambridge Footlights Harry Porter Prize for *Cloying*, co-written with Jack Gamble. He is a member of Soho Young Writers Lab, the Southwark Playhouse Young Company, and recently completed an MA in Writing for Performance at Goldsmiths, University of London.

The Old Red Lion Theatre is a hotbed for the development of professional theatre where bold, dynamic and innovative work is created and seen first. We seek to nurture exciting new talent and consider the Old Red Lion to be an independent extended family of aspiring and ambitious theatre makers. This has included the likes of Kathy Burke, Nina Raine, Abi Morgan and Katie Mitchell, to name but a few.

In the past few years the Old Red Lion has transferred work both off-Broadway and to the West End on numerous occasions. Recent productions include: *The Complete Works of William Shakespeare (Abridged)*, the longest-running ever off-West End comedy play; *Kissing Sid James* (London and off-Broadway); *The Importance of Being Earnest* (Old Red Lion Theatre and Theatre Royal Haymarket); *Mercury Fur* (Old Red Lion Theatre and Trafalgar Studios) and *The Play That Goes Wrong* (Old Red Lion Theatre, Trafalgar Studios and No. 1 UK tour).

Executive Director
Damien Devine

Managing Director
Helen Devine

Artistic Director
Stewart Pringle

Associate Director
Nicholas Thompson

Bar Manager
Tony Curran

Events Manager
Joe Devine

Literary Manager
Ben Weatherill

Piranha Heights in rehearsal.

Above: Rebecca Boey (Lilly).

Below: Jassa Ahluwalia (Garth).

Opposite page, top: Jassa Ahluwalia (Garth).

Middle: Ryan Gerald (Medic).

Bottom: Jassa Ahluwalia (Garth), Rebecca Boey (Lilly), Ryan Gerald (Medic).

Special Thanks to

ROOM ONE

for providing excellent rehearsal space

Room One . . . 'a space to create', is located in historic Clerkenwell, the heart of London, for centuries a hive for artistic and intellectual radicals. Room One takes its name from the original teaching room used by Yat Malmgren, one of the most influential practitioners of the twentieth century. Upon his retirement in 2001, Malmgren chose James Kemp, Training Director and co-founder, to inherit his work and was keen that it find a permanent home. Room One will soon be launching a residency programme and a membership scheme, aimed at artists from across the different disciplines. Resident Artists will be afforded full use of our space and materials in aid of their artistic evolution. Room One's Studio and Gallery space is also available for hire (you can find more information about this by visiting www.roomone.com/explorespace).

With over 4,000 square feet of creative space, Room One enables artists versed in various disciplines to form a greater aesthetic collective, allowing a complementarity between the arts and broadening the vision of each artist. With our Gallery, Studio and Study Centre, we are positioned to host numerous projects at any one time and believe that the interaction this will create will form the base for a stronger artistic scene in London and beyond.

Piranha Heights

For Lisa Goldman

Child Rowland to the Dark Tower came . . .
William Shakespeare

The lighthouse attracts the storm . . .
Malcolm Lowry

The whole of appearance is a toy.
Wallace Stevens

Piranha Heights was first performed at Soho Theatre, London, on 15 May 2008. The cast was as follows:

Alan	Nicolas Tennant
Terry	Matthew Wait
Lilly	Jade Williams
Medic	John Macmillan
Garth	Luke Treadaway

Director   Lisa Goldman
Designer   Jon Bausor
Lighting Designer   Jenny Kagan
Sound Designer and Music   Matt McKenzie

Characters

Alan
Terry
Lilly
Medic
Garth

The top-floor flat of a tower block in the East End of London.

Alan *(thirty-seven, tracksuit) is holding a feather duster.*

He is gazing up at an ornate crystal chandelier.

Slight pause.

He gets chair and (none too easily) stands on it.

Carefully, he starts dusting chandelier.

He's engrossed in this as –

Terry *(forty-two, leather jacket) appears at the open front door.*

He watches **Alan** *for a moment. Then –*

He flicks the light switch on.

The chandelier blazes!

Alan *cries out.*

Terry *laughs.*

Alan   Jesus!

Wobbles on chair.

Terry   Careful. Don't fall.

Alan   You could've fucking killed me.

Terry   Perhaps I *wanted* to fucking kill you.

Alan   Turn it off, Tel. I can't bloody see . . . where . . .

Terry *turns light switch off.*

Alan *is struggling down from chair.*

Terry   So what happened to you then?

Alan   Eh? What d'you mean?

Terry   I've been waiting for-fucking-ever!

Alan   'Waiting'? I *told* you it'd take me two hours to get here.

Terry   You did not. 'I'm in the car now,' you said. 'I'm on my way!'

Alan   On my way *to the airport*, I said. I was with a punter. I told you. By the time I get *there* and then drive all the way back *here* −

Terry   I didn't hear any of that.

Alan   Well, I said it.

Terry   Well, I didn't hear it.

Alan   Perhaps . . . you misheard or −

Terry   I didn't fucking mishear any −

Alan   The line was bad. Okay? Let's not argue, brov.

Terry   Who's arguing?!

Slight pause.

That feather duster suits you.

Alan *puts feather duster away.*

Terry   . . . So. Why'd you change it?

Alan   Eh? Change what?

Terry   The lock on the front door. You'll explain when you get here, you said. Or did I 'mishear' that bit too.

Alan   No, no. You heard right. Simple answer. After Mum died I couldn't find her keys. Searched everywhere. I was worried they might have fallen into the wrong hands. Probably hadn't. But . . . well, you can't be too careful, can you.

Terry   Jesus, Al.

Alan   What?

Terry   It took you this 'two-hour drive back from the airport' to think of that, did it?

Alan   I don't know what you –

Terry   Nothing to do with keeping me out, I suppose.

Alan   Keeping you – ? Jesus, Tel, why would I want to do that?

Terry   You tell me.

Slight pause.

It's cold in here. You got a window open?

Alan   No.

Terry   Perhaps it's Mum's ghost. You heard her dentures clacking?

Alan   Don't talk like that.

Terry   You know what this place needs? An exorcism.

Alan   Jesus Christ! Can't you just . . . for once . . . Let's be nice to each other, brov. Eh?

Terry   . . . Okay, okay.

Alan   . . . You've lost a bit of weight. You look younger. I'm jealous.

Terry   . . . You've lost a bit of weight too.

Alan   Really?! The doctor's put me on this new diet.

Terry   Lower that cholesterol, eh?

Alan   My veins are like shag-pile apparently.

Terry   Jesus.

Alan   I know.

Terry   We'll have to start hoovering you next, brov – ha, ha, ha!

Alan   Be more fun than a shower – ha, ha, ha!

Slight pause.

It's good to have you back, brov.

Terry   It's good to *be* back.

They are about to embrace as –

Lilly (*calling, off*)   Terry!

Terry (*calling*)   Yeah! He's here! Finally!

Alan   Who's that?

Terry   You'll like her – Oh! (*Calling*) My bag, Lilly! Don't forget my bag!

Alan   You didn't tell me you brought someone with you.

Terry   Didn't I? Perhaps I did but you didn't hear. Bad line, you said. Right?

Lilly (*jumbled clothes, face covered with scarf*) *rushes in.*

She gazes at flat.

Terry   Well? What d'you think?

Lilly (*in 'foreign' accent*)   Zip-a-dee-doo-dah!

Terry   I think she likes it.

Alan   Who the . . . who the fuck is this?

Terry   Lilly.

Lilly *has picked up ornament.*

Alan   Put that down! – I'm supposed to avoid stress, Tel.

Terry   Lilly's not stress.

Alan   Down, I said.

Snatches ornament from her.

Lilly   Talabanski!

Terry   She can touch what she likes, Al.

Lilly (*at* **Alan**)   Ha! – Zip-a-dee-doo-dah! Zip-a-dee-doo-dah!

Starts spinning around chanting 'Zip-a-dee-doo-dah!'

Alan   What's she doing?

Terry   She's happy.

Alan   She's a fucking lunatic.

Terry   Why don't you just go home.

Alan   I'm staying right here.

Lilly *grabs* **Terry**'s *hands.*

They both start spinning and chanting.

Alan   There's things we need to – Tel! There's things we need to discuss.

Terry   *What* things?

Alan   Jesus! You're gonna break something in a minute. This is me avoiding stress, is it? I'm on medication, you know. I'm a heart attack waiting to happen.

Terry *staggers into sideboard.*

Alan   There! What did I tell you? Eh?

Straightens things on sideboard.

Terry *and* **Lilly** *have stopped spinning and chanting.*

They are laughing.

Alan   This is Mum's stuff, Terry! *Mum's!* You have no right to come back here with some . . . some stranger and – Are you drunk? Is that it?

Terry   Haven't touched a drop in thirty-nine days.

Alan   Oh, yeah, sure. (*At* **Lilly**.) Approve of alcoholism, do you?

Lilly   Noshti shem allah.

Alan   Yeah, yeah, whatever – I've driven like a bat out of bloody whatsit to meet you here and all you can do is –

Terry   Hell.

Alan   Eh? . . . What?

Terry   Bat out of.

Lilly   Hell!

Slight pause.

Alan   Brov . . .

Terry   What?

Alan   As I . . . as I said on the phone I'm glad you've come back because . . . well, I want to . . . I need to . . . to have a little talk with you about . . . I . . . I need to . . .

Terry   *What*, for fuck's sake?

Alan   I can't think with her looking at me!

Lilly   Zarak!

Terry   She's not going anywhere, Al.

Alan   Mum wouldn't want her here.

Lilly   Be polite!

Terry   You hear that? And relax, for fuck's sake. Think of your heart. Okay. So. Brother dearest . . . what is it you wish to discuss? Speak. You have my undivided attention.

Alan   . . . As you know . . . the Housing Association –

Terry   Flowers!

Alan   Eh? What?

Terry   Bag! – Lilly?!

Lilly   Yoshti!

*Gets **Terry**'s bag.*

Alan   Terry?

Terry   It's Mother's Day, Al.

Alan   I'm aware of that. Why d'you think I brought the roses?

Indicates vase full of red roses.

Terry   Well, let me show my respect for our poor departed mum too.

Gets twigs and weeds from bag.

Alan   Oh, no! Weeds, Tel? *Weeds?!*

Terry   Picked them myself.

Alan   Where from? The fucking rubbish tip? Oh, they stink!

Terry *has gone to vase.*

Alan   Don't! I've only just put my flowers in there.

Terry *takes flowers from vase.*

Alan   You fucking bastard! – Stop it! *Stop!*

Terry *and* **Alan** *struggle over vase.*

Terry   It's what Mum deserves, Al! Twigs and weeds!

Alan   Roses! Mum deserves roses!

Lilly   No violence!

Tries to separate them.

Terry   Twigs and weeds!

Alan   Roses!

Terry   Weeds!

Alan   Roses!

Lilly   No violence! No violence!

Terry *stops struggling, laughing.*

Alan   Everything's a fucking joke for you!

Terry   *You're* a joke!

Alan   Yeah?

Terry   Yeah!

Alan *puts his flowers back in vase.*

Lilly *is picking up twigs and weeds.*

Terry   Mum always said you had no sense of humour.

Alan   She didn't.

Terry   'Alan's got no *joie de vivre*.'

Alan   Mum never said '*joie de vivre*' in her fucking life.

Lilly   Lishtwala?

Indicates twigs and weeds.

Terry   Over there, Lilly. Please.

Indicates sideboard.

I'll arrange them later. *When we're alone.*

Alan   Why you doing this? Eh? You . . . you fuck off to God knows where for seven fucking weeks. Not a word to anyone. I had to handle everything by myself. Mum's funeral. The eulogy – that should've been *your* job. And now you just . . . you just stroll back like nothing's fucking happened . . . It's not fair, Tel. It's not fair.

Slight pause.

Lilly (*at* **Terry**)   . . . Terry, yakety yak Shangri La, Alan.

Slight pause.

Terry   . . . What's on your mind, brov?

Slight pause.

Alan   . . . As you know, Mum had written a letter to the Housing Association saying she wanted this flat to pass on to her son.

Terry   Me.

Alan   The Housing Association's not sure.

Terry Oh?

Alan *gets letter and pen from drawer.*

Alan They'd like us to sort it out between ourselves. Legal.

Givers letter to **Terry**.

Alan So if you could just pop your name there, brov.
Thank you.

Terry *tears up letter.*

Terry Shove it. Up your. Arse.

Alan But the Housing Association –

Terry Don't bullshit me, Al. I'm not one of your sheep-
brained morons from the minicab office – He thinks I'll just
sign my rights away.

Alan But the Housing Assoc –

Terry Don't! I'm warning you. This flat can be passed on
once. The eldest son has first choice. And who's the eldest son,
I wonder? Oh! It's me! This place is mine, Al. *I* know it. *You*
know it. Lilly knows it – Don't you, Lilly?

Lilly Yoshti.

Alan But . . . you don't *need* this place. *I* do.

Terry What d'you fucking *need* it for? You've got a house
with . . .

Slight pause.

Oh . . . hang on, hang on! Light bulb above head. Ping! . . .
You're going to leave Sylvia!

Alan . . . Wh-what if I am?

Terry Ha! *Now* I get it! A ready-made flat. No hassle.
Shazam!

Alan It's not like that.

Terry   He's never had the guts to do it from scratch, Lilly.
Oh, no. But this – You fucking coward!

Lilly   Coward!

Spits.

Alan   Oi! We don't spit here.

Terry   Listen, Alan. You want to leave your wife? Fine. But
do it properly! Get a place of your own. Or set up somewhere
with one of your ditsy bimbos.

Alan   What 'ditsy bim –'?

Terry   But don't – *don't!* – come running back to Mum's like
a . . . a dog to its fucking vomit.

Alan   Like you, you mean.

Terry   I don't want this place for *me*. I want it for *her*.

Points at **Lilly**.

Terry   This girl has suffered.

Lilly   Malala!

Terry   Tell him!

Lilly   Lilly Dad head cut off. Lilly Mum stone to death. Lilly
suffered big. Bigger you ever suffer. You suffer tiny spark.
Lilly suffer atomic.

Terry   And she's got a baby.

Lilly   Bubba!

Terry   Helpless baby Bubba.

Alan   . . . Where is it?

Terry   Eh?

Alan   'Helpless baby Bubba'.

Lilly   Bubba at park with Medic.

Alan   Medic?

Terry   Her partner.

Alan   Jesus Christ! You gonna have the whole fucking family here?

Terry   They can have Mum's room.

Alan   'Mum's – '? Oh, you evil sod.

Terry   *Evil?*

Alan   You know what Mum's last words were? *Your name.* She was begging to see you. I phoned you. Didn't I? I pleaded with you to come. Pleaded. Mum died not hearing you say, 'I love you, Mum.' She heard *me* say it. She heard Garth say it. She even heard *Sylvia* say it. But *you?* No! And now you'll never have the chance. Because Mum's gone, Tel. She's dead! *Dead!*

Terry *runs to bathroom, retching.*

Lilly *rushes after* **Terry**.

Alan   Make sure he gets it down the toilet. I don't want any mess.

His mobile rings.

(*Into mobile.*) Hello, Husbands of Stupid Fat Ugly Wives Club . . . Oh, where's your bloody sense of humour? . . . Well, who's stopping you? Just don't make a mess, love, eh? No razors. And whatever you do, don't hang yourself. Your weight, probably bring the whole fucking roof down. What d'you want anyway? . . . A car?! Where'd Garth get a fucking car from? Jesus! Listen, stay out of his way till I get back. You'll only provoke him . . . You *do*, Sylvia. You provoke Garth. You provoke *me*. Tell you, if they put you in a room with the Dalai fucking whatsit he'll be shoving a broken beer bottle in that fucking fat mush of yours before you have a chance to say Hari cunting Krishna – Eh? . . . I'm at Mum's. Guess who's back – Oh! And Sylv, no mention of Terry to Garth, eh . . .

Cos Uncle Terry's hardly the best role model for the kid right now, is he, you stupid bucket of pig spunk . . . Oh, boo-hoo.

Hangs up.

Lilly *has come out of bathroom.*

Lilly   This place . . . Zip-a-dee-doo-dah!

Alan   Yeah, yeah, so you keep saying.

Lilly *picks up small framed photo.*

Lilly   This Alan?

Alan   . . . Yes.

Lilly   Alan pretty boy.

Alan   Handsome.

Lilly   Washti nosh?

Alan   Girls are pretty. Boys are handsome – And stick to English please!

Lilly   Alan wearing . . . football uniform?

Alan   . . . Yeah.

Lilly *studies photo more closely.*

She starts laughing.

Alan   What's so bloody funny?

Lilly   Alan legs.

Alan   What's wrong with my bloody – ? Give it here!

Snatches photo from **Lilly**.

Alan   I was on the school team. A scout had spotted me. I had a future.

Puts photo back in place.

Lilly   . . . Alan not in football future now?

Alan   No.

Lilly   Why?

Alan   I . . . I broke my leg. Last game for the school and . . . well, it healed wrong and −

Lilly   That why Alan cripple.

Alan   I'm not a . . . Jesus! I've got a slight limp, that's all − Your fucking accent. Where you from?

Lilly   Oh . . . Lilly from far, far away.

Alan   Well, 'Lilly' don't sound a 'far, far away' name to me.

Lilly   It short for something much longer. Too complicated for your Cockney tongue. You say it − You strangle yourself.

Alan   Try me.

Lilly   . . . Lillyespidoshushinopolusskallyfragielippyiskidova.

Alan   . . . Oh. Right.

Lilly *gazes at large, golden framed photo on wall.*

It is of **Alan** *and* **Terry** (*as children*) *with Mum.*

Lilly *points at photo.*

Lilly   Alan . . . Terry.

Alan   What? Oh! . . . Yes.

Lilly   Terry *very* handsome boy.

Alan   So everyone kept telling me.

Lilly   Terry *still* very handsome now. Alan *not* still handsome now.

Alan   . . . Please don't feel you have to make conversation.

Lilly *points at photo.*

Lilly   Mum.

Alan   Yes.

Lilly   Mum very . . . hygienic.

Alan   'Hygienic'? Well, she was clean and smart, if that's what you mean. Mum – she never left the flat with a hair out of place. The neighbours admired her for it. They looked up to her. When she bought a new piece of furniture neighbours used to come up to see it – That chandelier! I was with Mum the day she bought it. We were down the market. Me, Mum and Terry. Mum saw it in a shop window and – Hang on, hang on!

Flicks the light switch on.

The chandelier blazes.

Lilly   Oh! Zip-a-dee-doo-dah!

Alan   'That's the kind of thing to make a statement in our new flat, don't you think, boys?' Terry whistled when he saw the price tag. Me and Terry had to carry it home. You can imagine the size of the box. It wasn't so much heavy as . . . well, we had to be careful. It's a fragile thing. 'Make sure you don't break anything, boys.' Mr Samuels – he's dead now, used to live down the corridor – he fixed it up for us. When Mum turned it on for the first time – We all gasped! Me and Terry thought it looked like a UFO. We'd lay underneath it and make out we were stranded aliens about to be rescued by the Mother Ship.

Slight pause.

Lilly   . . . How Mum exploded?

Alan   Explode – ? Jesus. Mum wasn't bloody exploded.

Lilly   Bombs explode here.

Alan   I know that, yes, but –

Lilly   One at supermarket. Suicide bomb. Little boy die.

Alan   Yes, yes, I'm aware of that. But Mum . . . she wasn't . . .

Lilly   Mum hang herself from lemon tree?

Alan   No. Jesus. Mum – she just went to sleep and . . . her heart stopped.

Lilly   Heart stop without anyone making it stop?

Alan   . . . Yes.

Lilly   Shazam!

Terry *comes out of bathroom, wearing a woman's pink bathrobe.*

Terry   Reborn!

Alan   Oh, take that off.

Terry   I've puked over everything, Al.

Alan   Jesus. Everything you fucking touch – (*At* **Lilly**.) That last day. When I phoned to tell him we'd lost Mum. He trashed the place. You know that?

Terry   He exaggerates.

Flicks light switch off.

Alan   He pulled that down!

Points at chandelier.

Terry   It was an accident.

Alan   How do you pull a chandelier down by accident?

Terry   I was changing a bulb. I was drunk.

Alan   Alcoholic! What did I tell you!

Terry   Yes! *Then* I was! But *now* I'm not!

Alan   You've been an alcoholic since you were thirteen.

Terry   I was *not* drinking when I was thirteen, Al.

Alan   Oh! I imagined Mum cleaning up all those piles of vomit, did I?

Terry   Once! *One* pile. And *not* when I was fucking thirteen.

Alan   Lots of piles. When you were thirteen. Younger!

Terry   Oh, you're just making things up.

Alan   I am not!

Terry   You are!

Alan   I'm not!

Terry   You are!

Lilly *strolls out of flat.*

Alan   Wh-where's she . . . ? She gone?

Terry   Popping back to her squat probably.

Alan   'Popping back to her – '?

Terry   Mr Samuels' old flat.

Alan   Whoa! Whoa! Are you telling me . . . ? You ran away from here and ended up making friends with someone who's squatting in Mr Samuels' old flat?!

Terry   No. I made friends with her here.

Alan   Wh-when?

Terry   About an hour ago.

Alan   An *hour*!

Terry   Lilly walked past when I was trying to get in the flat. Took me back to hers while I waited for you. See, Al? If you hadn't've changed the lock . . . Oh, sweet mystery of life . . . How's Garth?

Alan   Eh? What?

Terry   Garth. Fifteen. So high. Calls you 'Dad'.

Alan   He's fine.

Terry   How'd he handle losing Mum?

Alan   He handled it. We *all* handled it. Without you.

Terry   Any more . . . trouble?

Alan   Don't know what you mean.

Terry   Al.

Alan   I am not discussing my son's problems with you. That's if he's got any problems. Which he hasn't.

Terry   No more . . . animal stuff?

Alan   What animal stuff?

Terry   Has he hurt any more animals?

Alan   That was an accident.

Terry   You don't Sellotape a snake to a bar in an electric fire and turn it on by accident, Al.

Alan   There's nothing wrong with Garth. Anyway, he's on new medication. He's getting my full attention from now on.

Terry   The Prince of Too Late!

Alan   I'm gonna give him a new home.

Terry   A new – ? Oh! *Now* I get it. You don't want this place for *you*. Oh, no. It's for Garth. Is that what you're telling me now?

Alan   Him and me.

Terry   Jesus.

Alan   It's what Mum wanted.

Terry   You sicken me, Al. You know that?

Alan   *What?*

Terry   You've *never* taken any fucking interest in that kid.

Alan   I have.

Terry   Wanna know what your idea of being a parent was?

Alan   Not really.

Terry   Plonk Garth in front of a telly and make him watch cartoons all day.

Alan I never *made* him do anything. He *loved* cartoons.

Terry The same one? Over and over?

Alan Kids do that.

Terry What was it now? – *Pinocchio!*

Alan It's a bloody good film.

Terry You never played with him. You never took him anywhere –

Alan Okay, okay, enough.

Terry 'You should never have had children, Alan.'

Alan Mum didn't mean it like that. She meant I should never've had them with Sylvia.

Terry Everything's Sylvia's fault, eh?

Alan No. I've made a few mistakes.

Terry 'A *few*?'

Alan At least *I'm* trying to put things right. What's *Sylvia* doing? Eh? Laying in bed stuffing her face with kebabs and Prozac all day. What kind of an example is that for Garth? Eh? Tel, I've got to get him away from her. Start again. Please . . . *Please.*

Terry . . . It's too late, Al.

Alan 'Too late'?

Terry You. Garth.

Alan But I –

Terry *What?* You think you can just flick a switch and turn fifteen years of Unhappy Party into Happy Party? Eh? Well, I'm sorry, but it don't work like that. Not in families. You've been a shit father and that's shit that sticks. There's not enough air-freshener in the world to make things sweet between you and your son.

Alan   That's not true.

Terry   It is.

Alan   It's not.

Terry   It . . . *is*.

Alan   . . . It's . . . *not*.

Lilly *returns, holding bag.*

Lilly   Medic and Bubba not back yet – Where North Star?

Terry   Eh?

Lilly   North Star. Sky. For prayers.

Terry   . . . Oh! I see. Well . . . I'm not . . . (*At* **Alan**.) Where is it? You're the navigator.

Alan   I drive a cab not a fucking jumbo jet.

Terry   But you must have some general idea where –

Alan   That way! Towards the gasworks.

Lilly *takes gold lamé jacket from bag.*

She spreads it on floor and kneels on it.

Alan   What's she up to?

Terry   You heard. Prayers.

Alan   On a gold bloody jacket?!

Lilly   Elvis Presley jacket! Show respect!

Terry   Show respect, brov.

Lilly *has taken candelabrum from bag.*

She starts lighting candles.

Alan   Oh, no! Not candles! Mum hated candles.

Terry   Mum never said a word about candles.

Alan   'Dripping wax can ruin a carpet.'

Terry   Stop making things up.

Alan   I fucking heard her. 'Dripping wax can ruin a – '

Terry   Well, it's *my* carpet now and I don't care.

Alan   You don't care about *any*thing. That's your whole problem – Oh, Jesus!

Lilly *has taken sparkling tiara from bag.*

Terry   Respect, brov.

Alan   Respect!? For *this*? (*At* **Lilly**.) What's next? Three choruses of 'When You Wish upon a Star'?

Lilly *strikes a pose and –*

Lilly   O! Chirpy-chirpy-cheep-cheep.

Alan   Oh, give me a fucking break!

Terry   Come here, come here.

Pulls **Alan** *to one side.*

Terry   What harm's she doing? Eh?

Alan   But, Tel, this is –

Terry   None. No harm. In fact all she's tried to do since she walked in here is stop me and you killing each other – No, brov! Listen! Toleration. Freedom for people to worship how they choose. It's the mark of a civilised society.

Alan   It's the mark of a lunatic asylum.

Terry   You want my advice? Stop worrying about what *she's* doing and start worrying about what *you're* gonna do when you leave Sylvia and haven't got anywhere to fucking go.

Heads for bedroom.

Alan   'Haven't got anywhere to – ' But this flat is where I'll – Oi! Tel. Wh-where you – ? . . . Terry!

Terry   My room. Clothes.

Stares at **Alan**.

Terry   Alan? . . . What you . . . what you bloody gone and done?

Goes into his room.

(*From bedroom.*) No! My stuff!

Rushes out of bedroom and –

Terry   Where's all my fucking stuff gone?

Alan   The police said he could be dead, Lilly. Suicide.

Terry   I've been running away since I was fifteen. I've *always* come back – You *know* that.

Alan   It's gonna be Garth's room.

Terry   You had no right to even *go* in there. My work!

Alan   Drawing comics ain't *work*!

Terry   Graphic novels!

Alan   Kids' stuff.

Terry   I was on the brink of getting published.

Alan   You've been on the brink for twenty years – Know why he *stayed* on the brink? 'Terry's got talent, but everything he does is copied from other people.'

Terry   Mum never said that.

Alan   Know what one of his stories was about? This young bloke gets bit by a – wait for it! – radioactive donkey. I kid you not. And this bloke turns into . . . guess what? Donkey Man!

Terry   So?

Alan   It's a ripoff of the fucking Spider-Man plot. Even *I* know that.

Terry   It's an ironic homage.

Alan   Can you hear him? Eh? Mum always said that's why you started drinking. 'He'll never really achieve anything and deep down he knows it.'

Terry   You bloody bastard!

Alan   Yeah?

Terry   Yeah!

Alan   Yeah?

Terry   Yeah!

Alan and **Terry** *approach each other, threateningly.*

Lilly   No violence.

Terry   Alright, alright.

Paces room.

A new start. Right, Lilly?

Lilly   Yoshti.

Terry   We've got to . . . to let go of the past.

Lilly   Yoshti.

Terry   All the old grievances. The old sins. We've got to forgive them.

Lilly   Yoshti.

Terry   Wave goodbye to the past and don't look back and – Burn the bones!

Alan   'Burn the – ' (*At* **Lilly**.) What's he going on about?

Terry   It's what they did in medieval times. Midsummer's night. Old animal bones. They'd throw them on to a big bonfire and – the Feast of John the Baptist! That's what it was called. Everyone'd get drunk and they'd dance round the fire and . . . well, go crazy. Do all sorts of things they'd never normally do. They'd say they were tempted by fairies.

Lilly   Fairies?

Terry   Small. Wings.

Lilly   Locust.

Terry   Human.

Lilly   Human locust?

Terry   Look, all I'm trying to say is . . . Burning the bones –
It was a way of saying 'a new world has begun'. And that's
what we need here. A new world – Pray, Lilly. Please. Say
your wonderful words.

Lilly (*praying*)   O! Chirpy-chirpy-cheep-cheep! Tsunami Bali
ave maria Korea Allah akbar shoo-be-doo-bop spiritus sancti
Hallelujah fallujah chiquitita al jazeera. O! Chirpy chirpy
cheep cheep bin laden fee-fi-fo-fum Fernando torpedo disco
Shangri La eternitas shoo-be-doo-bop putin shoo-bee-doo bob
Assad etc.

Terry – *as* **Lilly** *prays – has gone to his bag and taken out jeans and
T-shirt.*

He takes off dressing gown.

Alan   Tel! There is a *girl* present!

Terry   She's not looking.

Putting on jeans and T-shirt.

Alan   It's not appropriate!

Terry   'Not – '? Oh, you're such a prig.

Alan   Prig?!

Terry   'Alan's such a boring stuffed shirt.'

Alan   'Boring stuffed shirt'?! Me?

Terry   You!

Alan   Mum would *never* say that.

Terry   She did.

Alan   She didn't.

Terry   She did.

Alan   She didn't.

Terry – *now dressed – has started picking up framed photos.*

Alan   Hey! What you . . . what you bloody doing?

Terry   Burn the bones, brov.

Alan   Burn the – ? Oh, no! No!

Terry   Out with the old!

Alan   That's family stuff, Tel. Mum! *Us!*

Terry   You want them? Here!

*Starts throwing photos at **Alan**.*

Alan   Don't! You're gonna break one of them in a minute.

Terry   You can take anything you want, brov. That fair?

Alan   I don't wanna *take* anything anywhere. It all belongs *here*.

Puts photos back.

Terry   Fucking propaganda – Oh! This!

Goes to golden-framed photo on wall.

Alan   Leave that alone!

Terry   Chairmum Mao!

Alan   Don't say that.

Terry *tugs at photo.*

Alan   It's screwed on!

Terry   Screwdriver!

Alan   We haven't got one.

Terry   Look at that face, Al.

Alan   Eh?

Terry   Our beloved mother.

Slight pause.

You'd never believe it of her, would you.

Alan   Believe what – ? Oh, no. No!

Terry   Kingsmead Estate.

Alan   Don't start all this again.

Terry   What do you remember?

Alan   I'm not doing it.

Terry   What do you – ?

Alan   Nothing, for fuck's sake. I was only four when we moved out.

Terry   Seven. I was twelve. What do you remember?

Alan   I'm not listening!

Terry   You must remember *some* thing!

Alan   You don't stop, do you. On and on. 'Terry's like a woodpecker when he wants something. Peck, peck till he gets it.'

Terry   What do you remem – ?

Alan   Woody Woodpecker!

Terry   What do you – ?

Alan   Peck, peck.

Terry   What do – ?

Alan   Peck –

Terry   Alan!

Alan   The wallpaper in our bedroom! Knights in armour or something.

Terry   Richard the Lionheart.

Alan   And that's it. Nothing else.

Terry   You don't remember the broken windows?

Alan   No.

Terry   Dog turds through the letter box?

Alan   No.

Terry   We had them.

Alan   Really.

Terry   Yes. Know why?

Alan *doesn't answer.*

Terry   Do you? Know? Why?

Alan   I do not. *Want.* To know!

Terry   When we lived on Kingsmead Estate –

Alan   Don't, Tel. Please.

Terry   When we lived –

Alan   Peck, peck!

Terry   Our mum was a prostitute.

Lilly *stops praying.*

Alan (*at* **Lilly**)   Ignore him. It's all lies.

Terry   Neighbours forced Mum out.

Alan   She *wanted* to move out.

Terry   Bollocks.

Alan   She wanted a new start after . . . after Dad died.

Terry   After Dad . . . *what*?

Alan   . . . He was dead as far as Mum was concerned.

Terry   He left us because Mum was a –

Alan   Why're you doing this? What's the point?

Terry   Mum kept whoring when she was here.

Alan   My tendons are like piano wires! Look!

Terry   How d'you think we got the best bathroom in the block?

Alan   The workmen loved Mum.

Terry   Oh, they 'loved' her alright.

Alan   *Respected* her – She was the first person to move in, Lilly. Workmen were still laying concrete.

Terry   Leave her out of it!

Alan   You invited her in! – Mum went down to the basement one day. A workman took his jacket off so she could kneel and put her handprints in the wet cement. Like in Hollywood.

Terry   The only thing true about that is Mum on her knees with a bunch of men.

Alan   Your mind's a fucking sewer.

Terry   What about the jewellery?!

Alan   *What* fucking jewellery?

Terry   The gold rings and stuff men gave Mum.

Alan   Why would men give Mum their 'gold rings and stuff'?

Terry   When they didn't have cash to pay for –

Alan   Mum's jewellery box is still on her dressing table. Empty!

Terry   I know that, for fuck's sake! It's me who'd been living here for the past two years, don't forget.

Alan   Only because you had nowhere else to go.

Terry   'Nowhere else to – '? I had a flat in New Cross!

Alan   A *room* in a flat. That he couldn't afford.

Terry   Not true – He's lying.

Alan   You owed six months' rent!

Terry   Lies. All lies.

Alan   It was *me* who paid the bloody bill.

Terry   This is a fantasy, Alan. Jesus. I should go to you for my plots.

Alan   You should go to *someone*!

Terry   Listen, you talentless tub of putrefied goose fat. You *asked* me to come back here – No! You *begged* me! – He *pleaded* with me to come back and look after Mum.

Alan   'Look after – '? Mum didn't need no looking after.

Terry   Mum had cancer, Al.

Alan   No.

Terry   How many tits did she have?

Alan   Jesus! The way he talks about her? His own mother!

Terry   How many?

Alan   I don't remember!

Terry   'Don't remem – '? You listening to this? He don't remember how many breasts his own mother had – I'll give you a clue. It was somewhere between none and two? Take a pot shot.

Alan   He makes a joke out of everything.

Terry   None! Zilch titties! Why? Double mastectomy.

Alan   She always looked fine to me!

Terry   Because every time you fucking came round – on those *rare* fucking let's-celebrate-and-have-a-party occasions – I'd spent half the fucking day preparing her. Enough drugs to stun an elephant. Buckets of make-up. Hours tweaking the wig.

Alan   Mum had lovely hair.

Terry   'Alan hates coming here. Illness disgusts him.'

Alan   Mum would never say that!

Terry   You broke her bloody heart.

Alan   Shut it, Tel.

Terry   She'd've lived longer if it wasn't for you.

Alan   Shut it before I –

Terry   You killed her!

Alan   Bastard!

Terry   Yeah?

Alan   Yeah.

Terry   Yeah?

Alan   Yeah.

Lilly   No violence!

Slight pause.

Terry   About five months ago I heard Mum get out of bed in the middle of the night. I found her at the top of the stairs. The wind was howling. Her nightdress – it's all flapping and she's sort of leaning forward like . . . like she's the figurehead of a ship. She's got this . . . this intent look in her eyes. Like she's listening to something. God was speaking to her in the howling wind of the stairway.

Alan   Stop it.

Terry   He was telling her the cancer could be cured. All Mum had to do was have faith.

Slight pause.

I found this evangelical group. Out at Stratford. Met every Friday evening. The service was led by this young guy. Jeff.

Very happy-clappy. Jeff called people up who needed to be healed. Mum didn't hesitate. Jeff – he put his hand on Mum's head. I wanted to rush up there and say, 'It's all gobbledegook! Don't be fooled by it, Mum!' But then I saw her face and . . . I'd never seen her look so turned on.

Alan   Don't be disgusting.

Terry   I took Mum there every week. No one ever offered to help us. Not so much as a lift in their car.

Alan   Friday's my busiest night.

Terry   Sin.

Alan   Wh-what?

Terry   That was Mum's favourite word now. Jeff gave her a Bible. She carried it everywhere. Mum learnt huge chunks. She'd seen the light and knew she was saved. She asked Jeff to save me.

Alan   You *need* bloody saving!

Terry   The night I hit her –

Alan   No! I don't . . . I don't wanna hear about . . . No, Tel!

Terry   We'd just got back from a religious meeting. Mum – oh, she was high on divinity. She could feel the cancer dissolving like a sugar cube in tea. She was sitting there.

Alan   No, no, please.

Terry   'What do you do when I'm asleep? I bet you sneak out to have sex with men.' 'Chance'd be a fine thing, you selfish, hypocritical bitch. I'm looking after you twenty-four fucking seven. I reek of your shit. Your medicine. Who'd wanna come anywhere near me, let alone suck my fucking dick?' 'You need to ask God to forgive you! You need to – ' She's off on one now. Dentures clacking. And I hated her. Hated her so fucking much. It was like a . . . like a monster on the bottom of an ocean. There! And Mum's words – they're echoing down from above and waking it up. An eye's opened!

Red. The monster's moving now. Mouth opening. Teeth large as bread knives. Its tail goes swish and – up! The monster's swimming up! Up to the surface. There's gonna be a mighty fucking sea-burst. There's gonna be an explosion. There's gonna be – 'Bitch!'

Strikes out at the air.

Alan   You bastard! She was doing all right till you did that.

Terry   No!

Alan   Her own son hitting her. She never got over it – It was *you* who killed her!

Terry   You bastard!

They struggle.

Terry   *You* killed her.

Alan   *You* killed her.

Lilly   No violence.

Terry and **Alan** *still struggle.*

Terry   *You* killed her.

Alan   *You* killed her.

Lilly   No violence.

Gradually, she parts them.

Pause.

It's getting darker outside now.

Terry *turns lamp on.*

Slight pause.

Terry   . . . I saw an angel.

Alan   Wh-what?

Terry   In a car park.

Alan   Wh-what you talking about?

Terry   Three days ago – no, four. Night. I'd gone to the back of the hostel.

Alan   What fucking hostel?

Terry   The hostel Jeff runs in Stratford.

Alan   Jeff? Oh, Jesus.

Terry   Jeff don't like smoking in the hostel. I'd just lit up when – There! Something swirling and blue. Like a fragment of the Aurora Borealis. You know?

Alan   No.

Terry   The angel told me to go home. It wouldn't tell me why. But now . . . oh, now I know.

Alan   Why?

Terry   Lilly.

Alan   Jesus.

Terry   It's all part of God's plan – Pray with me, Alan!

Alan   What?

Terry   I want you to do it even if you don't want to do it.

Grabs **Alan***'s hand.*

Alan   You're scaring me now! – Don't!

Terry *is on his knees.*

Terry   Come on, brov!

Alan   My heart's a beehive of blood clots!

A rumble of thunder.

Lilly *cries out in panic.*

Terry   Lilly?

Alan *and* **Terry** *stop struggling.*

Alan   What's wrong with her?

Lilly   They explode!

Terry   She thinks it's bombs.

Lilly   Explode Lilly!

Terry   No, Lilly. No. It's thunder. That's all.

Lilly   Door! It break and fall. Men With Mask stand in no-door place. They have gun. They have knife.

Terry   It's alright . . . Shush, now, shush.

Lilly   Men With Mask say to Lilly Dad, 'You cut hair of men too short. Now we cut barber head.' Knife slice Lilly Dad throat. Blood splash like red rose oil gush. Men With Mask pull Lilly Dad head. String of skin from head to body. Skin string go ping. Garden of blood blossom red rose lake. Men With Mask say Lilly Mum show too much skin. They put Lilly Mum in hole. Lilly Mum like human tree. Men With Mask throw stones at Lilly Mum. Red blossom on human tree. Tree fall. Lilly runs. Men With Mask catch Lilly. First Man With Mask get on top of Lilly. He stick cock in Lilly. Lilly scream. Second Man with Mask stick cock in Lilly mouth go to hell and rot forever –

Medic (*off, faint*)   Lilly!

Lilly   Medic!

Rushes out of flat.

Pause.

Terry   . . . You seen the sky?

Alan   What?

Terry   The sky. Look.

Alan   I know what the sky bloody looks like.

Terry   Not this one. It's like . . . like the end of the world. 'The Earth also was corrupt before God, and the earth was filled with violence.'

A rumble of thunder as –

Medic   Oh! Yess!

Lilly *is entering, pushing a battered pram.*

Medic (*sixteen, shaven, tattooed*) *is with her.*

Wind howls in the corridors of the tower block.

Medic *and* **Lilly**   Zip-a-dee-doo-dah!

Alan   Jesus! (*At* **Terry**.) You happy now?

Medic   Who's this one?

Lilly   Alan.

Medic   Bad Neighbour!

Alan   Wh-what?

Medic   You didn't want my Lilly here. That's bad in my books. Stay out of my sight cos you're likely to light my fuse – Shut the door, Lilly.

Lilly *shuts front door.*

Howling stops.

Terry   Welcome, Medic!

Medic   Oh, Lilly. This is him, right?

Lilly   Yoshti.

Medic   Good Neighbour!

Hugs **Terry**.

Medic   You're right, Lilly. You can feel the goodness in him. It's like touching a microwave. Show me your hands, Good Neighbour.

Looks at **Terry**'s *hands.*

Medic   Bet he can heal the sick – Can you, Good Neighbour? Can you heal the sick?

Terry   I don't think so.

Medic   Have you tried?

Terry   Well . . . no.

Medic   He ain't fucking tried, Lilly. You've gotta *try*, Good Neighbour. Next time I'm out I'm gonna find you a real crippled cripple. One of those spaghetti-legged, toffee-toothed spastic fuckers, and I'm gonna bring them back here. I bet you – I *bet* you, Good Neighbour, you listening? – if you put your hands on him . . . these beautiful fucking hands – that spazz'll be dancing and – Lilly! Know what I expected to see on his hands? Nail holes! Cos you're like Jesus to me and Lilly, Good Neighbour. Cos Jesus said 'Love your neighbour' and gave them fish and bread and – Oh, fuck! Where's my manners. Introductions! I'm Medic.

Medic *grabs* **Terry**'s *hand and shakes it.*

Terry   Terry. I'm so glad to meet you, Medic.

Medic   You don't think I'm rude, do you, Good Neighbour Terry? Forgetting my manners like that.

Terry   Course not.

Medic   Cos I'd kill myself if you did. I'd grab a length of razor wire and I'd swallow it and then I'd yank it back up with all my guts stuck to it if you thought I was – (*At* **Alan**.) I don't like the way you're looking at me, Bad Neighbour.

Lilly   Shangri-La, Medic.

Medic   He's lighting my fuse, Lilly – If I was Vesuvius you'd be Pompeii. Know what I'm saying, Bad Neighbour.

Approaches **Alan**.

Medic   Feel my flow? My pyroclastic flow?

Lilly   No violence!

Medic *stops.*

Terry   Al . . . why don't you . . . you –

Alan   I'm not leaving.

Medic   No?

Lilly   Medic!

Terry   Al . . . Mum's room! There must be stuff you want to take home with you. Why don't you get it?

Medic   Yeah, fuck off to Mum's room, you Fuse-Lighting Cunt.

Slight pause.

Alan *goes to Mum's bedroom.*

Medic   Fuck me. Sorry. My fuse nearly lit up there, didn't it, Lilly. Been controlling it so carefully. Then I lose it in front of a . . . a Gandhi Saint Mother Teresa of Calcutta Princess Diana sort of person like you, Good Neighbour. I'm ashamed.

Terry   Don't be.

Medic   I am! I feel like killing myself. You got a food processor, Good Neighbour? I wanna stick my hands in it and mince them to stumps so I bleed to death. It's all I'm good for.

Terry   No, Medic, no.

Goes to embrace **Medic.**

Medic   Don't! I'm not fucking worth a hug. Don't even look at me. I'm an undigested peanut in a pile of puke.

Stands in corner, facing wall.

Terry   Medic . . . oh, mate . . . I used to have a terrible temper too, you know. I know what it's like.

Medic *turns to face* **Terry.**

Medic   You do?

Terry   Of *course* I do, mate. You take it out on other people but really . . . it's yourself you're beating up. Right?

Medic   No.

Terry   It is, mate.

Medic   It's not.

Terry   Mate, you don't *really* want to hurt other people, do you?

Medic   Yeah.

Terry   You don't.

Medic   I do.

Terry   No, no. You're doing it because –

Medic   I like hurting people.

Terry   Listen to me. You're only doing it because –

Medic   A telly!

Rushes to television and hugs it.

Medic   Oh, telly! Hello, telly.

Lilly   Medic love television.

Medic   Oh, it's a long time since I've had my arms round a telly. Oh, feel how smooth it is. Smell it! Pure telly! Oh, this'll be a good home for Bubba, Lilly – Bubba! Lilly, get Bubba! Fuck me, my manners have been well and truly blitzed to buggery today.

Lilly *has got a plastic baby doll out of pram.*

Medic   Good Neighbour Terry, this is my son –

Lilly   Mish!

Medic   *Our* son. Bubba. Say hello, Bubba.

Lilly *rocks the doll.*
It goes 'Mama!'

Lilly   Oh, Bubba!

Medic   Bubba's a bit of a mummy's boy is little Bubba. And why shouldn't he be? He's got the most beautiful mum in the whole fucking stinking shithole of a cosmos.

Lilly   Shem acushla, Medic.

Medic   Don't get embarrassed, Lilly, it's true – Don't you think she's beautiful, Good Neighbour Terry? – Show him your face, Lilly.

Lilly *looks away.*

Medic   Don't be shy. Good Neighbour Terry's family now – You won't be tempted to rape her, will you, Good Neighbour?

Terry   . . . No.

Medic   Why? You saying she's an ugly cunt or something? Eh?

Gets knife from pocket.

Why won't you rape her? Eh? Eh?

Terry   I . . . I . . .

Medic *relaxes and starts laughing.*

Medic   I got you going there, didn't I. Eh?

Puts knife away.

Terry   . . . Yes.

Medic   Ha! I've got a good sense of humour, ain't I? I could be on telly I reckon. Saturday night. Prime time. I'm a born entertainer, me – Lilly, show that mush! Hey, that'd be a good name for a game show. You can have three girls all in veils and stuff. And you have to guess what one's the dog. And when the contestant's made his choice the game show host says to the girl chosen, 'Tracy', or whatever her name is, 'Tracy! Show that mush!' Like it, Good Neighbour?

Terry   Well . . . I . . .

Medic   It's a fucking hit, I reckon – Come on, Lilly! Show that mush!

Lilly *still looks away.*

Medic   The audience is waiting.

Terry   If she's not ready to –

Medic   Shut it! – Come here, Lilly!

Slowly, **Lilly** *goes to* **Medic***.*

Medic *goes to reveal her face.*

Lilly *flinches away.*

Medic *stops.*

Slight pause.

He goes to reveal her face again.

She stays still.

Medic *reveals* **Lilly***'s face.*

Medic   Look at that, Good Neighbour. Have you ever seen such a Mona Lisa Marilyn Monroe Blessed The Holy Virgin Mother mush. Eh?

Terry   You have a lovely face, Lilly.

Medic   Those eyes. Those lips – fuck me! They're the kind of lips make you wanna shove your cock between them and spunk your load.

Lilly   Shish neiri.

Medic   She can't take compliments.

Lilly   Shish alal shem Bubba.

Medic   Oh! Sorry – I used rude words in front of Bubba, Good Neighbour Terry. I'm a rubbish dad.

Lilly   Medic good dad.

Medic   Don't look at me. I'm not worth it.

Goes to face wall as –

Lilly   Noshti! Noshti! – Medic teach Bubba things. Medic knows lots.

Medic *turns to face them again.*

Medic   I do! I'm well informed – Ask me something, Good Neighbour Terry!

Terry   Well, I . . . I don't know if I can just –

Medic   I'll *tell* you stuff, then. Tromp oil means trick of the eye. There are five hundred and seventy-eight calories in a whisky and lemon cheesecake. Ninety-five per cent of the universe is dark matter that we cannot even see.

Lilly *claps.*

Lilly   Bravo! Bravo!

Medic   I'm teaching little Bubba everything I know, Good Neighbour Terry. He's light years ahead of his age group already. Watch this – Little Bubba, what relation was the Blessed Virgin Mary to Our Lord and Saviour Jesus Christ who was nailed to a cross for our sins?

The doll goes 'Mama'.

Medic   How's that?

Terry   Very clever.

Lilly   Professor Bubba!

Medic   That's what we've got planned for our Bubba, Good Neighbour Terry. He's gonna go to university and learn every fact there is. He's gonna get himself so clued up he's gonna make Albert fucking Einstein look like a spastic with his head kicked in. You know what his specialist subject is gonna be, Good Neighbour Terry, Little Bubba's. Do you? Eh? Eh?

Terry   No.

Medic   Horology. Do you know what horology is? Do you? Eh? Eh?.

Terry   No.

Medic   The science of measuring time. And Bubba's gonna do more than just *measure* it. Oh, yes. He's gonna *travel* in it. You hear what I'm saying, Good Neightbour Terry? I am talking time travel – Look at his face, Lilly. Good Neighbour Terry don't believe me.

Lilly   Bubba laugh.

Medic   Good Neighbour Terry don't know how clever you are, does he, Bubba?

Lilly   Really clever Bubba.

Medic   Bubba's gonna invent this time machine and all three of us are gonna – Vissshhh! Back in time. Guess to when, Good Neighbour Terry?

Terry   Oh, I . . . I don't know –

Medic   Guess.

Terry   I really can't.

Medic   Try.

Lilly   Give contestant clue.

Medic   . . . Sixteenth of August 1977.

Terry   . . . I'm still not sure –

Medic   You ain't trying hard enough!

Lilly   Clue!

Medic   . . . Graceland.

Terry   Grace – ? . . . Oh! That's Elvis, right?

Medic   He's warm. Ain't he, Lilly?

Lilly   Warm.

Terry   It's where he lived.

Medic *and* **Lilly**   Warmer.

Medic   And?

Terry   Where he . . . died . . .

Medic *and* **Lilly**   Hot!

Terry   Or . . . *did* he die?

Medic *and* **Lilly**   Boil!

Medic   We're gonna get into this time machine – it better have a telly in it, Bubba, else Daddy'll get the right arsehole – and we're gonna go back to that date and that place and we're gonna solve one of the biggest fucking mysteries humanity had ever had to deal with. Namely –

Medic *and* **Lilly**   Is Elvis really dead?

Medic   Lilly prays to Elvis.

Terry   I've seen, yes.

Indicates gold lamé jacket.

Medic   That's the very jacket that Elvis wore at the Chicago International Amphitheatre concert in 1957 – Right, Lilly?

Lilly   Yoshti.

Terry   The . . . very jacket?

Medic   You doubt my word, Good Neighbour Terry?

Terry   . . . You're honest in your heart and I admire that.

Medic   I detect a certain patronising tone, Good Neighbour.

Terry   I would never –

Medic   I stole that jacket from Elvis Museum in Las Vegas.

Terry   You've been to Las Vegas?

Medic   I've been everywhere – Right, Lilly?

Terry   Yoshti.

Medic (*at* **Terry**)   Name a place.

Terry   Oh, I don't think it –

Medic   Name a fucking place!

Terry   Paris.

Medic   Been there. Another.

Terry   Baghdad.

Medic   Been there.

Terry   Aleppo.

Medic   Where?

Terry   Aleppo.

Medic   Been there. More than once – Do you think Elvis is God, Good Neighbour Terry?

Terry   Well, I . . . I can see how some people could worship him, yes.

Medic   That's not what I asked.

Terry   . . . I'm sure he's in heaven.

Medic   You're tap-dancing near the burning flames of heresy – Don't you think so, Lilly?

Lilly   Terry acushla Oxbridge, Medic.

Medic   You think?

Lilly   Yoshti.

Medic   She says you need to be educated in the sacred texts of the Memphis pretty boy. We'll start with 'Love Me Tender', shall we?

Terry   Let's do it later. But, yes. I'd like that. After all, love's what it's all about, right?

Medic   What what's all about?

Terry   . . . Life.

Medic   Oh. That – Any little niggling mysteries from the past you'd like to solve, Good Neighbour Terry?

Terry   Eh? What?

Medic   If you had a time machine. Any niggling little mysteries?

Terry   Oh . . . I'm . . . I can't think . . .

Medic   Fuck me, you must have *one* little niggling mystery! Jesus. Everyone's got at least *one* fucking little niggling mystery. You a retarded spastic or something?

Terry   . . . I'd like to find out what happened to my dad.

Medic   How d'you mean?

Terry   He left us.

Medic   When you say 'left' you mean –

Terry   He walked out on us, yes. When me and Alan were kids.

Medic   The fucking irresponsible cunt! I'd like to know where he is too. Know why? So I can ram a glass bottle up his arse then jump on his guts so it turns his intestines to mincemeat.

Lilly   Medic!

Medic   I'm sorry, Lilly, I'm sorry. But I can't help it. To leave your own flesh and blood. How can a dad do that? I could never walk out on my Bubba. Or my Lilly. I'd rather get a gallon of bleach and squirt it up me arse till I shit out me guts like fried tomatoes. Just the thought of going a day without seeing my Lilly and my Bubba – Just an hour! A minute! A second! I couldn't do it. – Oh, fuck, I'm getting all emotional now. It's stupid.

Terry   It's not stupid at all, Medic.

Medic   Don't look at me! I'm not worth it. I'm undigested sweetcorn in an icky-sticky turd.

Terry   No! It shows what a caring person you are.

Medic   Glad you said that, Good Neighbour Terry. Most people – they don't see it. Oh, sure I've carved up my fair share of faces. Who ain't? But underneath it all I'm as soft as a bag of tits.

Terry   I know you are.

Medic   I'm gonna be the best dad Bubba could ever have. Don't matter how young I am.

Terry   How old are you, Medic? If you don't mind me asking.

Medic   Two years and seven months.

Terry   Seriously.

Medic   I am two years and seven fucking months! I don't joke about time-related subjects. Horology is Bubba's vocation. I was washed ashore on a beach. Brighton. You know Brighton?

Terry   I've been there, yes.

Medic   You know that bit with the broken glass and blood?

Terry   Well . . . I can't say I recall that exact –

Medic   My birthplace. Where were you born?

Terry   London Hospital.

Medic   I've had stitches there. I ripped them out. Remember that, Lilly?

Lilly   Shem noshit chim.

Medic   Chim?

Lilly   Chim noshit cher-oo.

Medic   Cher-oo?

Lilly   Chim cher-oo.

Medic   Chim-in-ey.

Lilly   Yoshti! Cher-oo chim-in-ey.

Medic   Yoshti, yoshti.

They both laugh.

My stitches happened *before* I met Lilly. I'm always making mistakes like that. Know why? It's hard to imagine a time when I didn't know Lilly. It's like she's been with me ever since I was a slippery seaweed-sucker on the shingly beach of Brighton. You understand that, Good Neighbour Terry?

Terry   Oh, yes.

Medic   Once . . . before Lilly . . . my life was . . . well, it was shit. You know what I'm saying?

Terry   Yes.

Medic   And then one day . . . I turn round and I see . . . This perfect thing. This miracle. And my life changed. Once I was a broken bird on a beach but now . . . now I'm a flock of fucking flamingos.

Medic *and* **Lilly** *kiss.*

Alan *comes out of bedroom, holding photographs etc.*

Terry   Young love, Al.

Medic   Oh, here he is. The Fuse-Lighter Cunt. Look at him. Shaking like a chihuahua in a cement mixer – Fuck me! Lilly! Hide your beautiful face. You don't want to make this cunt all horny. He'll be getting his cock out and pearl jamming up your chocolate starfish before you can say . . . say . . . Fuck! I can't fucking think now! That's *your* fault, you Fuse-Lighter Cunt!

Lilly   Kiss Bubba.

Medic *kisses Bubba, then –*

Medic   Come and play with your dad, Bubba. Take his mind off the Fuse-Lighter Cunt.

Alan *heads for front door.*

Terry   I can help you carry some stuff, brov.

Alan   I don't want your help!

Terry   You . . . you going back to your place now or you − ?

Alan   There's still stuff here I want. That's mine!

Indicates golden-framed photo on wall.

There's a screwdriver in the car. I'll get it and −

Medic   Just fuck off!

Throws Bubba in the air and catches him.

Oh, he likes that, don't you − Weeeee!

Lilly (*with* **Medic**)   Weeeee!

Alan *leaves.*

Medic *nearly drops Bubba.*

Lilly *screams.*

Medic   Oh, Bubba . . . Bubba. You scared your dad there, Bubba. If anything happened to Bubba his dad would . . . would − oh, Bubba!

Lilly *and* **Medic** *kiss Bubba.*

Terry   Medic! Lilly! . . . Can I say a few words? Is that okay?

Medic   Say what you like, Good Neighbour Terry.

Terry   Will you . . . will you sit down, please?

Lilly *and* **Medic** *sit.*

Terry   Okay . . . well . . . first of all I'd like to welcome you all . . . both of you −

Medic   *Three* of us.

Indicates doll.

Terry   . . . I hope we can share in . . . share in . . . well, everything really. We shall learn from each other. That's what Jeff said. He's a good friend . A very good friend. Jeff says we have to face the truth about our lives before we can –

Medic   You're crap at this.

Lilly   Medic.

Medic   Well, he *is*!

Terry   Fair enough, mate. I probably am. But. . . . well, I've never done this before and I just wanted to . . . to elucidate –

Medic   Eluci-what?

Terry   Sorry, sorry. That's one of Jeff's words. 'The word of God will elucidate – '

Medic   But what's it fucking *mean*?

Terry   It means . . . to make things clear. So everyone understands. That's all I'm trying to do. Is that okay with you, mate?

Medic   It's fine. Just do it so it's fucking interesting – Hello, Bubba. Who loves you, eh?

Terry   Magneto!

Medic   What?

Terry   Magneto is the enemy of the X-Men.

Medic   He can twist metal with his mind!

Terry   You've read the comics?!

Medic   I've seen the films. We both have. Remember, Lilly?

Lilly   Yoshti.

Terry   Do you remember how he got his powers?

Medic   Who?

Terry   Magneto.

Medic   Er . . . No.

Terry   Shall I tell you?

Medic   Is it boring?

Terry   No.

Medic   Tell me then.

Terry   Auschwitz.

Medic   Gas chambers!

Terry   Yes! Very good.

Medic   We've seen that film too. Remember, Lilly?

Lilly   Noshti.

Medic   Yes, you do. It's about that concentration camp where they send all those actors. They divide them into two groups. Remember? The famous actors stay alive and the extras get gassed.

Lilly   Yoshti, yoshti!

Medic   She remembers now.

Terry   Auschwitz wasn't for gassing actors.

Medic   In the film that's *all* they gassed.

Terry   Just take my word for it. Okay?

Medic   . . . Okay.

Terry   So . . . Magneto gets sent to Auschwitz –

Medic   Because *he's* an actor.

Terry   No.

Medic   He is. I've seen the film with him in. He's played by an actor.

Terry   No, no. This is real life, Medic.

Medic   Magneto . . . in 'real life'?

Terry   Yes.

Medic   You sure about this, Good Neighbour Terry?

Terry   . . . Yes.

Medic   . . . Go on.

Terry   Magneto gets sent to Auschwitz. And he meets a girl there.

Medic   What was her name?

Terry   . . . Magda. They fall in love.

Medic   He gets his magnetic powers from her!

Terry   No, no. They survive Auschwitz and have a baby girl.

Medic   What was her name?

Terry   I . . . I forget.

Medic   Britney?

Terry   No.

Medic   Miley? Nicole? Kyra? Jade? Whitney? Paris? Estelle? Angelica? Sigourney?

Terry   Anya! So Magneto and his family live in this village. In Germany. And one day Anya is killed by a mob.

Medic   Why?

Terry   They . . . didn't like her.

Medic   Why?

Terry   Look, all you have to know is Magneto's daughter is killed and he's so pissed off about it that it wakes up all these magnetic powers inside him.

Medic   Fuck!

Terry So – and this is the point I've been trying to bloody make! – sometimes we think suffering has no purpose. We think of it as just . . . just . . .

Medic Suffering.

Terry But sometimes it can give us –

Medic Magnetic powers.

Terry Something positive.

Medic Bubba's crying.

Lilly Oh, sheishla slem, Bubba.

Medic Shishla shem, Bubba.

Terry Listen! I remember . . . I used to go to the canal. Down by the gasworks. One day . . . this bloke comes up. He's about thirty. Seemed really old to me. I was only fifteen. I said, 'I've escaped from an orphanage. The grown-ups hit me there. If I stay there I'll die.' The bloke takes me back with him. I stay a couple of days. I talk about this orphanage so much. It was all lies of course. But for me . . . it had become real.

Lilly and **Medic** *sing for Bubba to the tune of 'Twinkle, Twinkle, Little Star'.*

Medic *and* **Lilly** (*singing*)
  Salam, salam, Khamenei
  R'as as-sana niqabei
  Acuba acaba barakee
  Acuba acaba skaraskee
  Salam, salam, Khamenei
  R'as as-sana niqabei.

Terry (*as they sing*) The fantasies were easier because they helped me to avoid . . . all the things I couldn't . . . I was hiding! Hiding from what I didn't want to deal with. And we can't do that. We can't live fantasies.

Medic We can't – Can we, Bubba?

Terry   Learn from all my fuck-ups, mate. Please. I'm talking to both of you.

Medic   *Three* of us – Perhaps Bubba's hungry.

Lilly   Yoshti.

Terry   Look! No one's gonna be forced into it or rushed into anything. It will be in . . . in your own time. But I want us to at least agree. Agree we're gonna get on . . . on the journey to . . . to telling the truth about our lives and –

Medic *launches himself at* **Terry** *and grabs him.*

Medic   What you getting at? Eh?

Lilly   No violence!

Medic   We don't have to put up with this, Lilly. I can kill him easy. This flat will be ours.

Lilly   Falajarah shem shar Alan?

Medic   I'll kill *him* too.

Lilly   Alan shem shar *Sylvia*.

Medic   I'll kill *her*.

Lilly   Alan and Sylvia shem shar Garth.

Medic   Garth?

Lilly   Shem di Sylvia am Alan.

Medic   For fuck's sake! (*At* **Terry**.) How many family members you got, you fucking cunt!

Lilly   Come. We go now.

Medic   I can still smash his face in first.

Lilly   No violence – De-fuse, Medic!

Slight pause.

De-fuse now!

Medic *howls.*

Lilly   De-fuse more.

Medic *howls.*

Lilly   Shangri La nosh?

Medic *relaxes.*

Medic   Shangri La . . .

Lets go of **Terry**.

Medic   You pathetic little zarak!

Lilly *and* **Medic** *head for door.*

Terry   Medic! Mate! Don't . . . please.

Alan *enters, breathless, clutching screwdriver.*

Medic (*at* **Alan**)   You cunt!

Punches **Alan** *in face.*

Alan *crashes to floor.*

Lilly   Medic!

Medic *and* **Lilly** *walk out of flat.*

Terry   Al . . . you okay? – Here.

Helps **Alan** *to chair.*

He is bleeding.

Terry   Oh, Al . . . Just relax. Everything'll be okay.

Rushes to kitchen.

Gets some kitchen roll etc. as –

They'll be back. It's difficult at first. Looking truth in the face. It's painful. Like a birth. *I* know. *I've* been there. I'll give them a few minutes. Then I'll go down and have a chat. What d'you reckon, Al? A few minutes should do it, don't you think? Time to calm. See things a bit clearer. I blame myself, you know. Oh, yes . . . I was a bit . . . on the nose. You know me . . .

He has started wiping blood from **Alan***'s face.*

Terry   Any loose teeth, brov?

Alan *shakes his head.*

Terry   And your nose . . . ?

Feels **Alan***'s nose.*

Terry   Well, that's not broken.

Finishes wiping blood from face etc.

There! Good as new!

Takes kitchen roll etc. back to kitchen.

I don't think he meant to hurt you at all, brov. Not really. If someone like Medic *really* wanted to hurt you – Boy, you'd know about it. We'd be down the A&E by now. You'd be on life support. You know?

Comes out of kitchen.

Do you want something to drink? A cup of tea? Jeff's a big believer in the healing properties of tea.

Alan *shakes his head.*

Slight pause.

Terry   Al . . . I'd like to . . . I need to . . . to have a little talk with you about – Oh, I know this is not the best time and all that. But . . . well, there won't ever be a best time. Not for this. And . . . well, it's better to just say it all now. Is that okay with you, brov?

Alan *is staring at* **Terry***.*

Terry   . . . I want Garth to live here. With me.

Alan   . . . Wh-what?

Terry   Garth always loved this place.

Alan   I . . . I know that.

Terry   He calls it his sanctuary.

Alan   Why else d'you think I want him here? With me.

Terry   I want him to be part of the commune.

Alan   *'Commune'?*

Terry   Me, Medic, Lilly. Anyone who needs help.

Alan   Oh . . . no . . . No!

Terry   Garth needs someone to believe in him.

Alan   *I* believe in him.

Terry   The ship's sailed on that one, Al.

Alan   'The ship's sailed on – '?

Terry   Sailed and sunk. You cannot ignore your own child for fifteen years and then –

Alan   I've *never* ignored him!

Terry   Has he told you his Pinocchio Tree story?

Alan   Eh? What?

Terry   It takes place after the story of the Pinocchio we know. Okay? He's a real boy now. Flesh and blood and –

Alan   I know what a real boy's made of, for fuck's sake!

Terry   But something of his puppet days still remains . . . Guess what it is.

Alan   I'm not in the mood for –

Terry   His nose still grows when he tells a lie. And Pinocchio can't stop lying. Not big ones. But those little everyday sort of lies we all tell. Only now his nose is flesh and blood. Not wood. Little by little his nose grows. By the time his dad dies Pinocchio is an adult and he's got this nose that spreads all over his face and wraps itself three times around his body. And other parts of his body are growing too. Arms get longer and thicker. Fingers. Toes. Everything growing and growing. So Pinocchio starts wandering the world hoping to find the Blue Angel so she can cure him. For years and years he wanders. And still he can't stop lying. His skin and bones keep growing and growing. Walking gets more and more difficult. Finally, he can't move any more. He looks round him. He's in a forest somewhere. And then – a blue light! It's the Blue Angel. Pinocchio begs her to help him. She says, 'The only way to end your agony is to turn you back into wood.' And she waves her magic wand and – Pinocchio's wood! Only he's not a puppet now. He's a . . . Can you guess, brov?

Alan *just stares.*

Terry   He's a tree! Oh, it's so brilliant! And Garth reckons this tree is still out there somewhere. And if you lay underneath its branches and ask a question . . . a leaf will fall. And on this leaf will be written the answer. And it will be one hundred per cent truthful no matter how painful that truth is. Cos now – at last! – the Pinocchio Tree cannot lie. How's that? From your own son. Don't tell me you're not proud.

Alan   I've *always* been proud.

Terry   Brov . . . I want to be his Pinocchio Tree.

Looks at photo above mantelpiece.

Alan   Oh . . . no . . . no . . .

Terry   The truth about Mum – It'll set him free.

Alan   Garth *worshipped* Mum.

Terry   *That's* why he's got to know! He can't worship a lie.

Alan   . . . This ain't about helping Garth. It's about *you*!

Terry   No.

Alan   It's about *your* guilt. Making things easier for *you*.

Terry   Garth *wants* to live with me, Al.

Alan   Don't talk bollocks.

Terry   He told me.

Alan   When?

Terry   When I took him to the zoo.

Alan   Zoo! You never took Garth to no fucking zoo. Jesus!
Don't you think he'd've told me if you took him to the fucking
zoo? We tell each other things now. Me and Garth. Lots. Like
dads and sons should. He wouldn't've gone anywhere with you
without telling –

Terry *has taken photo from wallet.*

Terry   I didn't want to show you this.

Slight pause.

He hands photo to **Alan**.

Alan *stares at it.*

Slight pause.

Terry   That's a few months ago. A Sunday. I'd left Mum
with Jeff so me and Garth – we had the whole day to
ourselves. We're in front of the reptile house there. You see?
He loved the crocodiles. There were two baby ones. Garth
had tears in his eyes when he was watching them, Al. Tears!
Garth asked someone to take that photo. He asked them
calmly. Politely. Like the model son. We went for a bite to eat
afterwards. Garth talked intelligently – pleasantly – all night.
He joked with the waiter. He offered to pay. I said, 'Don't be
silly. This is my treat, son.' He said, 'Thanks, Dad.'

Alan   . . . No.

Terry   Look what he wrote on the back.

Alan *looks at back of photo.*

Slight pause.

Terry   I'm so sorry, Al.

Goes to touch **Alan**.

Alan *flinches away.*

Terry *puts photo back in wallet.*

Terry   Garth will live with me here. I'll be the parent he's never had. I'll tell him the truth about our whore of a mother. He'll make friends with Lilly. With Medic. I'll introduce them all to Jeff. The Holy Spirit will enter their lives. A new life will begin for them all. Reborn! Their old life will seem like a bad dream. *You* will seem like a bad dream . . . Now! I'll get the stuff you wanted from Mum's bedroom. The photos in the wardrobe, was it? And there's some of your old stuff under the bed. You want that? Course you do!

Goes into Mum's bedroom.

Medic *comes into flat.*

Medic   Where is he?

Alan *stares at* **Medic**.

Medic   Well?

A noise from Mum's bedroom.

Good! It's you I want to talk to. I'll be quick. Lilly sent me here for some peace negotiating. But there ain't no negotiating with a stupid prick like that. He's got that Hallelujah glint in his eye. Know what I mean? So fuck peaceful settlement – here's a new plan. Ready?

Alan *stares.*

Medic   Lilly says Good Neighbour Terry ran away. Police thought he might be a self-destruct. And if he was a self-destruct this place – it would all be yours. That's what you want, right? This place all for you. Don't bother to answer. I know it's what you want. Now – this is the important bit so listen very, very carefully – what if I was to tell you it could happen. Everything yours. Interested?

Alan *stares.*

Medic   Say you were to do a good deed. Like . . . well, set me and Lilly up in a little flat somewhere. It can be miles away from here if you like. You'll never have to see us again. The flat should be furnished, though. Big telly. Why, if you were to do a good deed like that . . . well, I'm sure a good fairy would come along and wave its magic wand and – Shazam! Know what I'm saying?

Alan *stares.*

Medic   I'll kill him. I'll do it now. It'll be over before you can say . . . whatever you want to say. Getting rid of the body won't be a problem. I'm mates with someone who's mates with someone who works in that pet-food factory in Peckham. Your brother'll be a hundred tins of Puppy Choice Juicy Nuggets by the end of the week.

Alan *stares.*

Medic   Well? What do you say?

Terry *(from bedroom, singing)*
    'In the sweet by and by
    We shall meet on that beautiful shore:
    In the sweet by and by
    We shall meet on that beautiful shore.'

Alan   . . . Do it.

Terry *comes out of Mum's bedroom, holding suitcase.*

Terry   Found this old suitcase, Al. Put all the photos in it and – Medic! Oh, it's good to see you, mate. We friends again?

Medic   Of course, Good Neighbour Terry.

Terry   I'm helping Alan sort out a few things he wants to take with him.

Medic   Don't let me get in the way, Good Neighbour Terry.

Terry   We'll talk once he's gone, yeah?

Medic   I look forward to it, Good Neighbour Terry.

Terry   Me too, mate – Come on, brov! Let's get this photo down.

Goes to large, golden-framed photo.

You hold, I'll screw – To coin a phrase. Ha, ha!

Medic   Ha, ha!

Terry *grabs hold of photo.*

Terry   Al?

Slight pause.

Alan *goes to* **Terry**.

Terry   . . . Hold it, brov.

Alan *holds photo.*

Terry *starts unscrewing photo from wall, his back to* **Medic**.

Alan *can see* **Medic** *over* **Terry**'s *shoulder.*

Medic *takes gun from pocket.*

Alan   No! No mess!

Terry   It's only a bit of dust, brov. We'll hoover.

Medic *puts gun away.*

He looks round flat.

He sees the pink dressing gown.

He takes belt from dressing gown.

He holds belt in preparation to strangle **Terry**.

He starts approaching **Terry**.

Unscrewing . . .

Closer . . .

Alan *takes photo off wall* –

Terry   Eureka!

Medic *wraps belt around* **Terry***'s neck.*

Terry *and* **Medic** *struggle.*

Alan *puts photo down.*

Medic *knees* **Terry***.*

Terry *collapses.*

Medic *tightens belt round* **Terry***'s neck.*

Alan *is becoming increasingly disturbed . . .*

He backs towards front door.

He is whimpering . . . on the verge of panic . . .

Terry *is struggling and gurgling . . .*

He is grabbing hold of furniture.

Things are pulled out of place.

A lamp is knocked over.

It flickers and crackles.

Garth *enters* (*jeans, T-shirt, black and acid green*).

He watches calmly as –

Alan *is slowly backing towards him.*

Medic *continues strangling* **Terry***.*

Alan *backs into* **Garth** –

Garth   Hi, Dad.

Alan   Garth!?

Garth   Hi, Uncle.

Alan *looks at* **Terry***, at* **Garth***, at* **Terry** *and* –

Alan   Jesus! No!

Rushes to **Terry** *and* **Medic**.

Alan   What . . . what's going on here!? Stop! Stop!

Struggles with **Medic**.

Garth *laughs*.

Alan   Stop!

Rushes to front door and –

Alan (*calling*)   Lilly! Violence! Help!

Medic   Leave her out of it!

Rushes to **Alan**.

Terry *falls to the floor*.

Garth *laughs*.

Medic *drags* **Alan** *back into flat*.

They are struggling.

Medic *hits* **Alan**.

Garth *laughs*.

Terry *is now back on his feet*.

He tries to help **Alan**.

They struggle.

Garth *laughs*.

Lilly *rushes in, holding Bubba*.

Lilly   No violence.

She puts Bubba down and joins the struggle.

More furniture is knocked out of place.

Another lamp is knocked over.

All lamps flicker and crackle.

Thunder and lightning.

Garth *continues watching.*

Then –

Alan *clutches his chest.*

He is in pain.

He falls.

Lilly   Alan!

Medic   Cunt!

Kicks **Alan***.*

Lilly   Alan sick!

Medic   Get him out my fucking sight, then.

Terry   Garth! Your Gran's room. Help.

Tries to get **Alan** *to his feet.*

Lilly   De-fuse, Medic. De-fuse!

Medic   It's hard, Lilly. Just looking at the fucking cunt –

Lilly   Don't look! De-fuse outside! Go! Go *now*!

Medic *rushes out of flat.*

Alan*'s legs give way.*

Terry   Garth!

Garth *doesn't move.*

Lilly *rushes to help* **Terry***.*

Terry   It's his heart, I think – Garth! Call an ambulance!

Garth *does nothing.*

Terry   It's all right, brov. Come on.

Terry *and* **Lilly** *take* **Alan** *to Mum's room.*

Slight pause.

Medic *howls, off.*

Slight pause.

Medic *howls off.*

Garth *howls.*

Terry *comes to bedroom door.*

Terry   You okay?

Garth   Yeah.

Terry   Ambulance?

Garth   Yeah, yeah, right away.

Takes mobile from pocket.

Terry *goes back into bedroom.*

Garth *puts mobile back in pocket.*

Slight pause.

Lilly *comes out of bedroom.*

Lilly   Water.

Goes to kitchen.

Medic *howls, off.*

Lilly *comes out of kitchen with water as –*

Garth *howls.*

Lilly *stops and looks at* **Garth**.

Slight pause.

Terry *comes to Mum's bedroom door.*

Terry   Lilly! Quick!

Goes back into bedroom.

Medic *howls.*

Garth *howls.*

Lilly *picks up Bubba.*

Terry (*from Mum's bedroom*)   Lilly!

Lilly *goes into Mum's bedroom.*

Medic *howls.*

Garth *howls.*

Terry *closes Mum's bedroom door shut.*

Medic *howls.*

Garth *howls.*

Slight pause.

Medic *comes into flat.*

Slight pause.

Medic *howls.*

Garth *howls.*

Medic *howls . . . it turns into a laugh.*

Garth *laughs.*

They both laugh.

Garth   He's de-fused now, Mr Green.

Medic   How'd'you know about de-fusing?

Garth   I heard Lilly say it.

Medic   You know Lilly?

Garth   I heard you say her name.

Medic   You pick things up quick – Hang on! Wh-who the fuck you talking to just now?

Garth   Mr Green.

Medic   Who the fuck's Mr Green?

Garth   Mr Green does not like bad language.

Medic   . . . Sorry.

Garth   Mr Green's my friend. He's a cricket.

Medic   Cricket? . . . You mean some sort of insect?

Garth   Correct. Have you ever seen *Pinocchio*?

Medic   That's a film, right?

Garth   It's set in Cartoon World.

Medic   Not seen it.

Garth   Mr Green is in that. He's called Jiminy Cricket in Cartoon World. But in all Non Cartoon Worlds –

Medic   Such as this one!

Garth   Correct. He prefers to be known as Mr Green – What's that, Mr Green?

Medic   What's he saying?

Garth   Mr Green wants to know if you've ever tried killing animals.

Medic   A few. Why?

Garth   De-fusing.

Medic   Please elucidate.

Garth   Next time try – what do you suggest first, Mr Green? . . . Excellent! Try treading on a terrapin. There's nothing like the sound of –

Medic   Cracking shell!

Garth   What's that, Mr Green?

Medic   What?

Garth   You can carry them round in a jar for emergencies. Same with lizards. And mice. Thank you, Mr Green.

Medic   Thank you, Mr Green – Why can't I see him?

Garth   Do you believe he's there?

Medic   Yes.

Garth   Then see him you will.

Medic   When?

Garth   When Mr Green decides it's time.

Medic   How much time, Mr Green? Eh? Eh?

Garth   He's by the bedroom door now. What's going on in there, Mr Green? . . . Yeah, yeah. I thought as much.

Medic   What?

Garth   Big fuss about nothing. Chest pains. Stomach cramps. Dad gets like this about once a week. Panic attacks.

Medic   What's Mr Green look like exactly?

Garth   Exactly?

Medic   Yeah.

Garth   . . . Green.

Terry *appears at bedroom door.*

Terry   Garth, what's the ambulance situation, mate?

Garth   Ten minutes.

Terry   They know where we are and everything?

Garth   Gonna call when they're downstairs.

Medic   I'll go down and meet them.

Terry   Thanks, mate . . . (*At* **Medic**.) You okay now, mate?

Medic   Never better. Sorry for trying to kill you and all that.

Terry   You wouldn't have killed me, mate. I know that. We'll talk about it later, yeah?

Medic   Look forward to it.

Terry   And . . . you two? Everything hunky-dory?

Garth   Hunky.

Medic   Dory.

Terry   Well . . . that's just . . . Couldn't be better! Talk, you two. Get to know each other. Go on.

Goes back into bedroom.

Medic   Cunt.

Garth   Cunt.

They laugh.

Medic   Where'd you meet Mr Green?

Garth   When I was born.

Medic   You remember being born?

Garth   Don't you?

Medic   Yeah. Of course. But most people don't.

Garth   What was yours like?

Medic   I opened my eyes . . . Seagulls. Ocean. Shingle.

Garth   Beautiful.

Medic   You?

Garth   Blood. Pain. Shit. I'm put into this glass container. Like a fish tank. I think, 'What am I? Why am I here?' And then – Mr Green!

Medic   You saw him?

Garth   He jumped on my fish tank.

Medic   Didn't he break it?

Garth   He's a teeny-weeny cricket, don't forget.

Medic   Of course! Teeny-weeny.

Garth   Teeny-weeny.

Medic   Teeny-weeny.

Garth   Mr Green said, 'You have been born for a very special reason, Mr Garth.'

Medic   What reason?

Garth   Shall we tell him, Mr Green?

Medic   Tell me.

Garth   Mr Green says to tell you but . . . where to begin, Mr Green? . . . Well, I've never really thought about it either . . . No, no, we need to start before that . . . Yes! Perfect!

Medic   What?

Garth   Broken glass!

Medic   Oh, yesss!

Garth   I'm five years old. Mum has just dropped a bottle in the kitchen . . . What? . . . Yes, yes, a wine bottle. Thank you, Mr Green . . . Of *course* the details are important, I agree . . . Mum drops a wine bottle. Smash! I pick up one of the pieces. About the size of a tooth. I run to the garden. I sit on the concrete. I look at the glass. And then I hear a baby gurgle.

Medic   Oh, yesss!

Garth   The next-door neighbour – what was her name, Mr Green? . . . Corrine. Mr Green remembers everything.

Medic   So do I. I'm well informed.

Garth   Corrine has come visiting Mum with her baby. I stand in the doorway to the kitchen. There they are. Mum and Corrine. And there – on the floor. In its little baby carrier. A wriggling bundle of skin. And that's when Mr Green tells me what to do.

Medic   Put the glass in with the baby.

Garth   I do.

Medic   Run outside.

Garth   I do.

Slight pause.

He makes sound of baby crying.

Medic   Yesss!

Garth   I run back to the kitchen and – oh!

Medic   Blood on the baby?

Garth   Blood on the baby.

Medic   Yesss!

Garth   Look at Mum and Corrinne.

Medic   Panic!

Garth   They are more alive than ever.

Medic   I see it in their eyes.

Garth   They're awake! For the first time in their lives.

Medic   They are!

Garth   And that's when I know!

Medic   What?

Garth   The reason that I'm here.

Lilly *rushes in.*

Lilly   Alan need tablets.

Gets tablets from **Alan***'s jacket.*

Looks at **Medic** *and* **Garth***.*

Slight pause.

Lilly   What . . . what happening here?

Medic   Happening where?

Lilly   You . . . Him.

Medic   Me? Him?

Garth   Him? Me?

Medic   You? Me?

Garth   Me? You?

Slight pause.

Terry *pops head in room.*

Terry   Lilly? You got them?

Lilly   . . . Yes.

Terry   Medic! You best be making your way downstairs, mate.

Medic   Fuck me, yeah, mate! Right away, mate!

Terry *goes back into Mum's bedroom.*

Lilly *gazes at* **Medic**.

Slight pause.

Lilly *goes into Mum's bedroom.*

Garth   Bleach!

Medic   Oh, yesss!

Garth   I'm seven years old. I swipe a bottle from home. I put it into this big mega water blaster thing I got for Christmas . . . Sorry, what? . . . Really? . . . No, no, of course. These things are important, I agree.

Medic   What?

Garth   Preparation details. The solution in the water pistol took a lot of experimentation to get right. Too much bleach and the liquid was too viscous to –

Medic   What's that mean?

Garth   Viscous? Thick. Like cat's blood twenty minutes after you've cut its head off.

Medic   Okay, right.

Garth   I couldn't get sufficient squirt power. And if there's too little bleach then there's sufficient squirt power but –

Medic   What's the point of squirting?

Garth   Exactly. In the end fifty-fifty seemed to do the trick.

Medic   I'll remember that.

Garth   I go to school with my mega bleach blaster.

Medic   Oh, yesss!

Garth   I look at my fellow students in the playground.

Medic   I hate them.

Garth   Me too.

Aims imaginary water blaster and –

Pow!

Medic   Yesss!

Garth   Pow!

Medic   Yesss!

Garth   Awake! Awake!

Medic (*with* **Garth**)   Awake!

Garth   No one's blinded.

Medic   Shame.

Garth   But there's lots of skin rash.

Medic   *Psoriasis!* That's a skin rash!

Garth   Their eyes were like squashed tomatoes.

Medic   Bet they locked you up.

Garth   I get away with it.

Medic   How come?

Garth   'I didn't know there was bleach in it. I filled it up from a bucket at home. Mum was cleaning the kitchen. Oh, I'm so sorry.'

Garth *and* **Medic** *laugh.*

Medic   Grown-ups are stupid cunts – Excuse my language, Mr Green.

Garth *goes to Mum's bedroom door.*

Garth   The ambulance is here, Uncle.

Terry (*off, from bedroom*)   Great! Good!

Garth   Is Dad okay?

Terry (*off, from bedroom*)   He'll be fine. Don't worry.

Garth   But I *am* worried, Uncle. It's my dad.

Terry (*off, from bedroom*)   I know, Garth. It's okay.

Garth *and* **Medic** *laugh.*

Garth   Being bad's a lot of fun.

Medic   Oh, such wise words.

Garth   Words I live by – Fire!

Medic   Yesss!

Garth   I've just turned fourteen. Dad's in the garage polishing his car. It's a new car. He loves his car. The car radio's playing. Dad's smoking. He's got a can of lager. I'm across the road watching him. I'm gonna steal some of his cigarettes. I'm waiting my chance. And then – Dad's going back into the house. I rush to the garage. There's his cigarettes. I take some out of the packet. And then I see . . . A canister of petrol. And what's this in my pocket?

Medic   Matches.

Garth   Everything lined up.

Medic   Like it's meant to be.

Garth   Fate.

Medic   Destiny.

Garth   Kismet.

Mimes striking match.

Medic *mimes striking match.*

Garth *mimes throwing match.*

Medic *mimes throwing match.*

Garth   Beautiful.

Medic   Ravishing.

Garth   We best get out.

Medic   Let's watch from across the road.

Garth   Good idea.

Slight pause.

There's Dad!

Medic   The garage is burning.

Garth   There's Mum!

Medic   I see her.

Garth   Neighbours.

Medic   They're all watching.

Garth   Look at their faces.

Medic   Awake!

Garth   Awake!

They 'watch' the fire.

Garth   . . . Mr Green, shall we tell him our plans?

Medic   Mr Green says yes.

Garth   You can *hear* him now?

Medic   A ravishing voice.

Garth   Indeed. Quite beautiful – That ignited petrol! I knew I had to make it happen again. Bigger. Much bigger.

Medic   You've made a fucking bomb.

Garth   Not yet. But I will. Lots of bombs. Mr Green has shown me how. I'm gonna make as many bombs as possible. And then I'm gonna put them where there are lots of people. And then – Boom!

Medic   Boom!

Garth   There will be many fatalities.

Medic   A great many.

Garth   A very great many.

Medic   A very, *very* great many.

Garth   But the ones who're killed are not important.

Medic   It's the ones who see the Boom that are important!

Garth   Correct. Some will see it in the flesh.

Medic   Correct. Some will see it on telly.

Garth   Correct. Those people who see the Boom either in the flesh or on telly –

Medic   Or any other way. Correct?

Garth   Correct. They will all be awoken and . . . Oh, tell him, Mr Green . . . Where . . . where are you? . . . Yes, yes, I can *hear* you but I can't – There you are!

Looks at chandelier.

Mr Green, will you tell Mr Medic exactly where the bombs will be put and exactly what will happen? You always explain things so much more exactly than me.

Medic and **Garth** *'listen to Mr Green'.*

They nod and give grunts of approval etc.

The wind howls.

They get more animated as it goes on and on.

They look at each other, giggling with excitement.

Then, starting softly and getting louder.

Garth   Boom.

Medic   Awake . . . Boom.

Garth   Awake.

Medic   Boom! Awake!t . . . Boom! Awake!

A flash of lightning and thunder.

Very loud and close now.

Garth *and* **Medic**   BOOM! AWAKE! BOOM! AWAKE! BOOM! AWAKE!

Medic   We've gotta do it! Me and you.

Garth   You and me?

Medic   Mr Green's nodding.

Garth   You can *see* him now?

Medic   He's wearing a . . . a . . .

Garth   On his head . . .

Medic   A hat.

Garth   Top hat.

Medic   Yeah. And smart clothes.

Garth   Waistcoat. And for when it raining –

Medic   His holding an umbrella.

Garth   You see it all, don't you.

Medic   I see what you see, Mr Garth.

Garth   I see what you see, Mr Medic.

Medic   I was nothing till I met you. I was a broken bird on the beach. But now I'm a flock of fucking flamingos.

They kiss passionately.

Lilly *comes out of bedroom, holding Bubba.*

Lilly   Medic, shelm Gomorrah shem.

Medic *and* **Garth** *separate.*

Medic   Eh? What's she going on about?

Garth   No idea.

Medic   Say something again, darlin'.

Garth   Yeah. Say something again, darlin'.

Medic   Say something again, darlin'.

Garth   Say something again, darlin'.

Lilly *stares.*

Medic   She's not speaking.

Garth   Perhaps she's been struck dumb.

Medic   By your beauty, Mr Garth.

Garth   By *your* beauty, Mr Medic.

Medic   *Your* beauty.

Garth   *Your* beaut –

Lilly   Shem allah talabanski!

Garth   Hang on. I think I . . . Yes! I recognise it now.

Medic   What is it, Mr Garth?

Garth   Gibberishki, I think.

Medic   You studied Gibberiski, Mr Garth?

Garth   I know a few phrases. (*At* **Lilly**.) Pronto shoo sluttsky!

Medic   Yeah – Pronto shoo sluttsky!

Garth   Pronto shoo sluttsky!

Slight pause.

Lilly   Medic, please . . . Bubba not want to stay here any more. We go, Medic! We go now.

Medic   Shoo.

Terry *comes out of bedroom.*

Terry   Medic? Thought you were going down for the ambulance, mate?

Lilly   No ambulance.

Terry   Eh? What's that?

Lilly   They lie. Look!

Terry   . . . Garth?

Garth *and* **Medic** *giggle.*

Terry   Wh-what's going on, guys?

Garth *and* **Medic** *stop giggling.*

They stare at **Terry**.

Slight pause.

Terry   Give me your phone, Garth.

Garth *backs away.*

Terry   This is no time for games.

Garth   He's annoyed, Mr Medic.

Medic   He is, Mr Garth.

Terry   Your dad's ill, for fuck's sake.

Makes lunge for the phone.

Garth *takes gun from pocket and aims it at* **Terry**.

Terry *freezes.*

Terry Jesus . . . Garth . . .

Garth Mum told me you were back.

Lilly Medic! Leave now!

Garth I came to say hello and welcome back.

Medic Hello and welcome back.

Terry It's okay, Garth. I understand.

Garth What d'you understand?

Terry I fucked off and you're annoyed with me. You think I let you down.

Garth You *did* let me down!

Terry Okay, okay, I did. I'm not denying it.

Garth I phoned you and phoned you.

Terry I threw my phone away.

Garth You knew my number.

Medic You knew his number.

Garth Why didn't you ring me?

Medic Why didn't you ring him?

Terry I . . . I'm gonna make it up to you.

Garth I don't want you to!

Medic He don't want you to.

Terry Let me explain.

Medic *hits* **Terry**.

Lilly No violence!

Garth Just tell me what you did with it?

Terry With what?

Garth The treasure.

Medic   Treasure.

Terry   Wh-what treasure?

Medic *hits* **Terry**.

Lilly   No violence!

Terry   Look! Let's . . . let's all calm down and have a nice cup of tea and –

Garth   Just tell me what you fucking did with it!

Medic   Tell him!

Terry   I don't know what you're talking about.

Garth   Did you spend it all?

Medic   You better not.

Garth   It was meant for *me*.

Medic   It was meant for *him*!

Strikes **Terry** *hard.*

Lilly   No violence!

Medic   If you was the *Titanic* I'd be an iceberg. Know what I'm saying? I'll sink you, Mister.

Garth   Sink you, Mister!

Medic   Sink you, Mister!

Terry   Please. I don't know what –

Garth   Gran told me about it.

Medic   Gran told him.

Garth   When she was in hospital.

Medic   When she was in hospital.

Garth   Gold rings and stuff.

Terry   'Gold rings and – '? You . . . you mean her *jewellery*?

Garth   Treasure!

Medic   Treasure!

Garth   Gran said she told you where it was.

Terry   Oh, no, no . . . Garth. Listen to me.

Garth   She said you had to spend it on *me*. To help *me*.

Terry   Listen. The jewellery she was talking about – it was a long time ago. Years. It was all sold and pawned. It's what paid for everything in the flat.

Garth   That's not what she said in hospital.

Medic   That's not what she said in hospital.

Terry   She was confused. All the morphine and the –

Medic   Liar!

Garth   Liar!

Lilly (*at* **Medic**)   Kiss Bubba.

Garth   She hid it in the chandelier, didn't she!

Terry   Wh-what?

Garth   That's why you pulled it down!

Terry   No!

Garth   Mr Green told me.

Medic   You bastard!

Strikes **Terry**.

Lilly   No violence!

Garth   Gran told me, 'I've saved the treasure for you and Mr Medic.'

Medic   I heard her.

Garth   Mr Medic was there.

Medic   I brought grapes.

Garth   What did you do with our treasure, you cunt?

Strikes **Terry**.

Lilly   Kiss Bubba.

Medic   Fuck off!

Pushes **Lilly** *violently away.*

Lilly *stumbles and falls.*

Garth *laughs.*

Lilly *pulls gun and aims it at* **Garth**.

Medic *draws gun and aims it at* **Lilly**.

Garth *aims his at* **Lilly**.

Garth (*at* **Lilly**)   Fuck off!

Lilly   Zarak!

Terry   Jesus! No. Keep calm. Everyone. Lilly . . . just get out!

Lilly   Lilly not go without Medic.

Medic   I've never fucking seen you before!

Lilly   Medic!

Garth   Where you from, darlin'? Hackney, darling?

Medic   Isle of Dogs, darlin'?

Garth   Bethnal Green, darlin'?

Medic   Somewhere near London Hospital, darlin'?

Garth   How near London Hospital, darlin'?

Medic   Accident and Emergency, darlin'?

Garth   Hurt yourself did you, darlin'?

Medic   Had your stomach pumped, darlin'?

Lilly (*without 'foreign' accent*)   No! Fucking don't!

Garth   Ooo, accent's slipping, darlin'.

Medic   Accent's slipping, darlin'.

Garth   What's your name, darlin'? Sharon? Emma? Iris?

Medic   No . . . Tracy. Tracy Wilmot.

Garth and **Medic** *laugh.*

Medic   From Wapping.

Garth and **Medic** *laugh more.*

Lilly   I'll blow your fucking brains out!

Aims gun at **Medic.**

Medic *grabs her hand (holding gun) and they struggle.*

Terry   Leave her alone!

Garth (*aiming gun at* **Terry**)   Don't move!

Medic and **Lilly** *are struggling very violently now.*

All remaining lamps are now knocked to floor.
They start flickering and crackling violently.

Lighting very skewed, distorting shadows.

Much screaming and shouting.

The thunder and lightning now reach their peak.
Howling reaches its peak.

It's as if the storm has entered the flat.

Lilly *seems to be getting the better of* **Medic.**
Garth *joins in the struggle.*

Lilly'*s gun goes off.*
Medic'*s gun goes off.*
Garth'*s gun goes off.*
All very rapid – bullet after bullet.

The chandelier – hit by bullets – falls. Many sparks.

Medic *pulls Bubba away from* **Lilly.**

Lilly   Bubba!

Garth *grabs hold of* **Lilly**.

Terry   No.

Garth (*at* **Terry**)   Don't move!

Aims gun at **Lilly**'s *head.*

Lilly   Bubba! Bubba!

Medic   It's a doll, you stupid cunt!

Lilly   It's not, it's not.

Medic   Look! Doll! Doll!

Lilly   Don't hurt Bubba!

The doll goes, 'Mama'.

Mum here, Bubba!

Terry   Give it back to her.

Medic *twists doll's arm.*

Lilly *screams.*

Terry   Jesus!

Garth   Where's the treasure?

Terry   There is none! Why won't you fucking listen to –

Medic *twists baby's arm again.*

Lilly *screams and struggles.*

Garth   You've got five seconds to tell me where the treasure is.

Medic   Then I cut the baby's head off.

Takes knife from pocket.

Lilly   No! No! – Tell him where it is! Tell him!

Terry   There's nothing to tell!

Garth   One . . .

Lilly   No! Medic good dad. Medic love Bubba.

Medic   Two.

Lilly   University for Bubba.

Garth   Three.

Lilly   Professor Bubba.

Medic   Four.

Lilly   Time machine!

Garth   Five.

Lilly   God!

Medic *starts hacking at doll's neck with knife.*

Lilly *starts screaming and struggling.*

Terry *goes to move.*

Garth *re-aims gun.*

Medic *continues to hack.*

Lilly's *screaming and struggling weakens.*

Medic *cuts head off doll.*

Lilly *stares, silent, broken.*

Garth *lets go of* **Lilly**.

Lilly *collapses to her knees.*

The storm is fading now.
Howling becomes less.
Lamps flicker less.

Slowly, **Lilly** *crawls forward.*
She picks up body and head of the doll.
She holds both bits very carefully, caressing them, kissing them.

Lilly   I'm gonna bury this one properly. Do you hear me?

She gets to her feet, cradling Bubba.

She heads for Mum's bedroom.

Terry   What . . . what are you? . . . You two . . . what?

Garth *and* **Medic** *look at* **Terry**.
Slight pause. Then –

Terry *makes dash for front door.*

Garth *and* **Medic** *grab him.*

They struggle.

Terry   No! No!

Alan *– very uneasy on his feet – appears at the doorway of Mum's bedroom as* **Lilly** *goes inside.*

Alan   Stop . . . stop . . .

Garth   Don't interrupt, Dad.

Terry   Alan! Help!

Alan *goes to the large, golden-ramed family photograph.*
He looks at the back of the photograph.
Several brown envelopes are Sellotaped there.

Garth *and* **Medic** *stop struggling with* **Terry**.
They are all watching **Alan**.

Alan   Your Gran got it wrong, son. She didn't tell your *uncle* where her jewellery was. She told *me*.

Removes envelopes from back of photograph.

He holds envelopes out to **Garth**.

Slight pause.

Garth   Mr Green . . . ?

Takes envelopes from **Alan** *and looks inside.*

Garth   Treasure!

Shows **Medic** *gold rings, gold chains etc.*

The howling has gone now.
The lights have stopped flashing.

Alan   I was saving it for you . . . us . . . So we can start all
over –

Garth *aims gun at* **Alan***.*

Terry   Jesus, Garth, it's your dad!

Garth   I ain't got no dad.

Slight pause.

I was born in the belly of a whale. An ancient whale full of
shipwrecks and shark bones. All these things sloshed around,
wore away, atoms of this, atoms of that. And then, one night,
lightning struck the whale and life sparked in this sloshing
subterranean stew. Just a tiny thing at first. No bigger than a
jelly baby – me! – floating in the guts of Leviathan. Over the
years I grew and I grew . . . Fingers! Hair! Teeth! And one
night the whale spouted me through the hole in its head and
I rode the surf like a dolphin till I was washed ashore. I crawled
across the shingle and wrapped seaweed round me to keep
warm. Seagulls brought me food. Bits of starfish and crusts of
bread. I played with shells and crabs. And, at night, the whale
sang to me from out at sea and I felt safe. I was happy there.
I belonged there. And that's when you found me. You took me
away from my beach. My true home. You took me to your
home in Dagenham and said I was your son. But you lied.
Everything you've ever said to me has been a lie. And now . . .
now there must be a sacrifice to appease the spirit of the
whale – now long dead – my true father.

Spins gun cartridge.

I've got one bullet in here. Whose skull it shatters don't matter
to me because both of you are lying cunts.

Aims gun at **Alan***.*

Terry   No . . . Garth . . . Not your own dad.

Aims gun at **Terry***.*

Alan   No . . . Please, Garth. Not your uncle.

Terry   Shut up, Alan.

Alan   It's me who let you down!

Terry   I let you down more.

Alan   No, I did. I did.

Garth *aims gun at* **Alan***.*

He pulls trigger.

It clicks but does not go off.

He aims gun at **Terry***.*

He pulls trigger.

It clicks but does not go off.

Garth *continues to do this.*

Alan *and* **Terry** *flinch and cry out.*

Click . . .

Click . . .

Alan *and* **Terry** *fall to their knees.*

Click . . .

Click . . .

Alan *and* **Terry** *curl up on the floor . . .*

Click . . .

Click . . .

Alan *and* **Terry** *are crumpled, helpless.*

Garth *lowers gun.*

Garth   No bullets left.

Medic *and* **Garth** *laugh.*

Alan   Garth . . .

Garth   Can you hear something, Mr Medic?

Medic   It's very faint, Mr Garth.

Garth   Look – these liars. They're fading.

Medic   Dissolving.

Garth   Like ghosts, Mr Medic.

Medic   Phantoms, Mr Garth.

Garth   And the flat – that's fading too.

Medic   Fading to nothing.

Garth   I can see right through the walls.

Medic   To the flat next door.

Garth   And the flat next to that.

Medic   And the flat below.

Garth   Below that.

Medic   Below that.

Garth   Below that.

Medic   Below that.

Garth   The car park!

Medic   And up! Look!

Garth   The sky.

Medic   Moon.

Garth   Stars.

Medic   The universe.

Garth   Beautiful.

Medic   Ravishing.

Garth   Ravishing.

Medic   Beautiful.

Garth   It's the end of the old world.

Medic   The birth of a new world.

Garth   Our world, Mr Medic.

Medic   Our world, Mr Garth.

Garth   Mr Green says we best get moving!

Medic   Of course, Mr Green.

Garth   We've got things to do!

Medic   Boom!

Garth   Awake! Boom!

Medic   Awake!

Garth and **Medic**   BOOM! AWAKE! BOOM! AWAKE!
BOOM! AWAKE! BOOM! AWAKE! BOOM! AWAKE!

They run out of flat.

Their 'booms' and 'awakes' fade.

Pause.

Slowly, **Alan** *goes to front door and closes it.*
The howling stops.

One by one, he puts the lamps back in place.
They stop flickering and stay on.

Alan   Kids, eh, Tel?

Terry   Who'd 'ave 'em, eh?

Alan   I know, I know. They got a bit carried away but . . .
they'll be back. Tails between their legs. And we'll give them a
hug and tell them everything's okay. What else can we do, eh?

He picks up twigs.

He puts twigs in vase with flowers.

Terry   Let me help you.

Alan   It's alright.

Terry   No, no, I want to.

Finishes arranging twigs in vase.

Alan *looks at the fallen chandelier.*

Terry *follows his look.*

Terry   We'll never fix it, will we.

Alan   I . . . I don't think so. Not now.

Slight pause.

Terry   Oh, God, Al . . . Mum . . . *Mum!*

Alan   Shush, now, shush. It's okay.

Terry   Did I kill her, Al? Did I?

Alan   No, brov, no . . . Did *I*?

Terry   Oh, no, brov. No!

They hold each other.

What're we going to do without her, Al?

Alan   I don't know . . .

Terry   H-how *can* we . . . carry on . . . ?

Alan   I don't know.

Terry   Nor do I.

A noise from Mum's room.

Alan   Did . . . did you hear that?

Terry   I did.

Alan   It came from Mum's bedroom, Tel.

Terry   I know, I know.

Alan *and* **Terry** *look towards Mum's bedroom.*

Terry   . . . Mum?

Alan   Mum?

Lilly *appears in doorway.*

She is wearing Mum's clothes.

Terry   . . . Lilly?

Alan   What . . . What're you wearing . . . ? Lilly?

Lilly   Lilly's gone, boys. It's Mum now – Oh, why the tearful faces? Tell your mum all about it. You know there's no problem your mum can't make better. Come on.

Alan and **Terry** *kneel at her feet.*

Lilly *strokes their hair.*

Lilly   Have faith in Mum, boys. Have faith.

The fallen chandelier glimmers and crackles.

Blackout.

Bloomsbury Methuen Drama Modern Plays

include work by

Bola Agbaje	Robert Holman
Edward Albee	Caroline Horton
Davey Anderson	Terry Johnson
Jean Anouilh	Sarah Kane
John Arden	Barrie Keeffe
Peter Barnes	Doug Lucie
Sebastian Barry	Anders Lustgarten
Alistair Beaton	David Mamet
Brendan Behan	Patrick Marber
Edward Bond	Martin McDonagh
William Boyd	Arthur Miller
Bertolt Brecht	D. C. Moore
Howard Brenton	Tom Murphy
Amelia Bullmore	Phyllis Nagy
Anthony Burgess	Anthony Neilson
Leo Butler	Peter Nichols
Jim Cartwright	Joe Orton
Lolita Chakrabarti	Joe Penhall
Caryl Churchill	Luigi Pirandello
Lucinda Coxon	Stephen Poliakoff
Curious Directive	Lucy Prebble
Nick Darke	Peter Quilter
Shelagh Delaney	Mark Ravenhill
Ishy Din	Philip Ridley
Claire Dowie	Willy Russell
David Edgar	Jean-Paul Sartre
David Eldridge	Sam Shepard
Dario Fo	Martin Sherman
Michael Frayn	Wole Soyinka
John Godber	Simon Stephens
Paul Godfrey	Peter Straughan
James Graham	Kate Tempest
David Greig	Theatre Workshop
John Guare	Judy Upton
Mark Haddon	Timberlake Wertenbaker
Peter Handke	Roy Williams
David Harrower	Snoo Wilson
Jonathan Harvey	Frances Ya-Chu Cowhig
Iain Heggie	Benjamin Zephaniah

For a complete listing of Bloomsbury
Methuen Drama titles, visit:

www.bloomsbury.com/drama

Follow us on Twitter and keep up to date
with our news and publications

@MethuenDrama

Printed in the USA
CPSIA information can be obtained
at www.ICGtesting.com
LVHW020845171024
794056LV00002B/406

9 781474 238847